ENLIVENING STORIES FOR MARRIED MEN AND WOMEN

ENLIVENING STORIES FOR MARRIED MEN AND WOMEN

Hemalatha Gnanasekar

KALPAZ

Enlivening Stories for Married Men and Women

Rs. 750

ISBN: 978-81-7835-833-8

Published in 2010 in India by
Kalpaz Publications
C-30, Satyawati Nagar,
Delhi-110052
E-mail: kalpaz@hotmail.com
Phone : 9212729499

Lasser Type Setting by: Rudra Computer Graphics, Delhi
Printed at : Chawla Offset Press, Delhi

*This is dedicated to
Shirdi Sai Baba, whose
blessings enabled me to
write this book*

Contents

Preface

This book is a collection of short stories for the married men and women. Marriage has its own twists and turns - some may be good, while others may be bad. The characters depicted in this book, through their actions, give you lessons for a smooth marital relationship. First and foremost amongst them is the truth that a willful hardheadedness will do more harm than good in marriage. The characters depicted in this book are wise enough. They learn to be cheerful and contented with their lot in life and do not kick against the pricks. They are good listeners, respect one another, have a good sense of humour and are willing to adapt and also accept the fact that you can't change your partner. In fact, through their actions, they teach you that for a happy marriage, it is not enough to simply adhere to the "give and take policy". They tell you that you need to go a step further and "give and only give".

After listening to her grandma's advice, Ramya besides giving up her judgemental attitude, also does not hold any grudges against her nitpicking husband.

In the story Fraud, you will appreciate that when Uma instead of covering over her sin, quickly asks for forgiveness from her spouse, Ganesh is willing to forgive her. For nothing is more important to a marriage than forgiveness and bitterness and unwilling to forgive will only end the relationship.

Though filled with pride, Rama the beauty queen is sensitive to her own failings! But ultimately she gives up her stubborn pride and becomes more understanding of and merciful towards her husband.

Nowadays, women all around are fighting for their rights and they no longer put up with the inhuman treatment meted out to them. They have proved that they can do anything they put their mind to. They are assertive and have become daring and take bold decisions in order to lead a life they aspire. You will also enjoy reading the stories of such audacious women who have succeeded in all aspects and have grown to be respected.

When Lakshmi loses her husband in middle age, life becomes dull and boring. However, she does not wish to sit and worry over the loss for the rest of her life. Find out how Lakshmi brings back meaning to her life in "Leap into the dark".

Sudha, unable to bear the frequent beatings of her husband who is a tormentor, walks out of the house, never to return. But one fine day, her husband calls on her and requests her to accompany him. Read the story "Tormentor" to know if Sudha changes her mind.

Her husband's addiction to the internet is getting on Neela's nerves. From the story "The Cyber Husband" learn how Neela brings about an end to his addiction.

After reading the fascinating stories in this book, you will also perhaps work to maintain harmony and experience the joy of reconciliation with your spouse. These stories are sure to enrich and enliven your married life.

1

The Fraud

Ganesh entered the room rather nervously. He had been a very shy person all his life and dared not look a girl in the eye, except his two sisters, for whom he had toiled all along his life, even sacrificing his own studies. After graduation, he had been interested to go to the States to develop his knowledge in Software Technology. Unfortunately, when he was doing his final year in college, his father passed away and being the eldest son in the family, the responsibility of getting his two sisters married fell on him. Abandoning the idea of going to the States, he now began hunting for a job. Since their mother had also left them years back, he had taken a vow of educating his sisters and also get them married. It took nearly ten years for his vow to be fulfilled and now that he was bereft of any responsibility and also well settled in a job, one of his Uncles settled his marriage with Uma. And today was his first night.

As he opened the door and stepped inside, he was delighted to see his bed decked with flowers. But his pleasure was short-lived, when he found the bride sitting in the corner of the bed sobbing ! Pulling a chair close to hers, he sat facing her. Trying to console her, he said, "I understand you are missing your family deeply ! You may feel free to share your thoughts with me. I can't bear to see you crying !" But the kind words only added fuel to the fire. Immediately, Uma got up and blurt out, "I don't like you ; nor am I interested in this marriage. My parents had forced me into this marriage without seeking my opinion." The sharp words pierced through Ganesh's heart. But somehow, he tried to retain his composure and maintain his cool.

Ganesh had witnessed many ups and downs in his life, but this was one knocking him down. He did not reply to her sharp words and calmly said, "Well if you don't like me, I can't help it. Whatever has happened to you, I am not responsible for that. You should have been bold enough and protested to your parents in the beginning itself. By being reticent, you have not only ruined your own life but mine too. Now that the marriage is over, you are helpless and so am I. As you have daringly conveyed your feelings to me, I promise not to bother you in any manner. You can chalk out the future plan for yourself and whatever be the decision you take, I shall abide by it."

Next day, his sisters left for their homes. Ganesh had not spoken a word to them about the last night. He did not wish to wound the feelings of his happy sisters. After seeing them off at the station, Ganesh returned and cooked food for the two of them. He asked Uma to join him for lunch and waited for her. But Uma was adamant and refused to eat anything. This provoked Ganesh. He told her firmly, "While you are free to take your own sweet time to chalk out your life in my abode, I don't like to see you sobbing all the time, refusing to eat anything. You can't die in my house starving like this. If you promise to eat something, you can stay here; otherwise I would have to inform this to your aged parents." Hearing this, Uma entered the kitchen and had her lunch.

Life had been indeed very cruel to Ganesh. From his childhood, he had been facing one storm after another. His mother left him when he was hardly five years old. His dreams of higher studies in the States had also been shattered with the death of his father, leaving him with a huge responsibility of taking care of his sisters. He enjoyed bringing up his obedient sisters but after their marriage, there was a great void in his life. To overcome his loneliness, he had agreed to the marriage proposal of his Uncle, even without seeing the girl. He was dreaming of a wife, who would take care of him with loving care ; but fate had dealt a severe blow to his life. Somehow, Uma's statement "I don't like you" had got well registered in his heart. Never did he feel the urge to ask her why she felt that way about him. To him, it did not matter anymore. Uma was now to him, just like another sister, cropped up from some remote corner of the earth – and it was his responsibility to at least keep her alive under his care, if not happy.

But God had been ruthless with Uma too. She was born in a middle class family and was the fourth and the youngest daughter in the family. Her parents were very strict and brought up their daughters in a disciplined manner. Her father was a Government servant. With the provident fund loans, he had settled the marriage of his three daughters amicably, as soon as they completed their schooling. However, when he retired from his service, he had a bulky amount with him. He did not wish to hurry the marriage of Uma who was hardly eighteen years old. He wanted to send her to a college. That was how Uma had been lucky enough to step into a college and enjoyed the laxity which was denied to her other sisters. She had also got a good job immediately after graduation in a reputed multinational company. That was when the real problem started.

It was hardly a week after she joined the duty, when she chanced to meet a smart young man. He traveled in the same bus, which she boarded everyday and got down two stops before hers. One evening Kumar introduced himself to her, telling that he also worked in the same organization where she worked and this was his first job. He had come all the way from Kanchipuram, leaving his parents all alone, just for this job. He further told her that he was presently staying in a hostel and would be pleased if she could find him a house with a low rent, as the rates were sky high in Chennai and the owners demanded a huge advance too. Uma promised to help him within a week's time. But on the same day itself, she found some time to telephone her college friend Arathi, whose father was in Real Estate business. Arathi was very helpful to her, for on the next day itself, she gave the address of a single bedroom flat, which was near her office. Uma then passed on the message to Kumar and introduced him to her friend. Thus blossomed her friendship with Kumar.

Everyday, they chatted for an hour in the bus stop. The friendly relationship slowly turned to love. On some days, they would skip office together and roam in the Marina beach or go out for a movie. Uma never had any reservations and spoke to him freely with an open heart. One Sunday morning, Uma told her mother that her boss had asked her to come to office, to clear off the pending works and went straight to Kumar's house. It was Kumar's birthday and he had invited her for a feast at Hotel Taj. After a sumptuous meal, they had gone out for a movie. And on that day, while parting, Kumar had expressed his wish to marry her.

Since then, Kumar started dropping her near her residence everyday, in his motorbike. Uma too, deluded her parents and visited his house on almost all Sundays. One particular Sunday, she told Kumar that she was feeling very sick drifting around like this and asked him to come home and meet her parents. But Kumar was reluctant and he promised to inform their love affair to his parents first and then send them on this errand. Generally, Uma would leave by afternoon, to join her parents for lunch but on that day, she continued to linger around in his house. Probably, it was the pleasant weather that prevailed on that day as the sun had disappeared all of a sudden and the weather turned cool. The dry leaves kept falling off from the trees and the breeze blew up the mud. It was as though a dust storm had started. Very soon, the clouds began to gather, resulting in a light drizzle. Within a few minutes, it resulted in a heavy downpour, and the place all around was filled with small puddles of water.

Uma began to feel the chillness. She wrapped her arms around her shoulders to keep from shivering. Kumar on noticing it, switched off the fan in the hall. But this too, was not helpful and Uma's teeth began chattering. Immediately, he took her inside the bedroom, where it was warmer, compared to the hall and asked her to relax a little. When her whole body was rocking, he decided to help her out. Using all his might, he began massaging the souls of her feet and palms and slowly her body warmed up and she stopped shivering. His touch sent tiny ripples down her spine and she wished he continued doing this to her. She lay there numb like a lifeless doll trying not to disturb him from whatever he was up to. Slowly, he was massaging her whole body and she never bothered to protest. Suddenly, when a thunder blasted, she clung to him, as if he was her life saviour and he lay down besides her soothing her fears away. Just then the power went out, and the place was in total darkness. Instead of lighting a candle, they continued to remain in darkness. The power returned within a few minutes, and the room was filled with a flood of light but by then, Uma had darkened her life for ever !

Later, she felt ashamed of herself for being unable to resist her bodily temptations. When she expressed her feelings to Kumar, he simply brushed it away by telling, "after all, we are going to be married shortly, so what is wrong in that ! Tomorrow, I am going to talk it out with my parents and bring them along with me and settle the marriage." And Uma was thrilled to hear the words from him.

On Monday morning, Uma was anxious to know the decision of Kumar's parents. But Kumar had not turned up to office that day. In the evening, she left early from office and went straight to his flat. Kumar was sitting on the sofa with a heavy book in his hand

and was deeply engrossed in it. On seeing Uma, he closed the book and apologized to her, "I was not able to go home yesterday. Just after you left that day, I received a letter by courier. It was from a company in States, asking me to attend an interview at Hotel Park Sheraton on the 15th of this month. I had, in fact, applied for a job in the States, a few months back, and now I have received a response from them. That is why I have taken a week's leave to put in all my efforts to get selected for the job." On hearing this, Uma was dumbfounded. But Kumar was quick to pacify her, "Very soon the two of us would be flying to the States."

From that moment, Kumar got himself busy with preparations. He had no time for Uma. Uma too, decided not to disturb his study. After a fortnight, Kumar turned up to office and Uma was happy to see him. Kumar informed her that he had got selected in the interview, and he was going to resign from his present job. He invited Uma to his house the next day to help him in packing up. The following day, Uma had gone to his house and offered her service. At the time of his leaving, Uma's eyes welled up and Kumar promised her that once he got settled in his new place, he would inform her his address and phone number. He also told her that he would appraise his parents about their love affair, before leaving for States and they would be coming to meet her shortly. Also, when he came to India for his vacation, he would wed her and take her along with him. At that time, her friend Arathi had also come there to give him a send off and Kumar, while handing over the keys to her, said, "I shall send you a cheque next month towards the rent which I am due to you." Then he took leave of them.

More than a month had passed and there was no response from Kumar. Life was miserable for Uma at home. In the meantime, her parents had consulted an astrologer as to when it was the right time to perform her marriage. The man after going through the horoscope said, "The auspicious time for her marriage is right away. If you don't conduct her marriage within a month, it would invariably get delayed for another three years." The words of the astrologer worried them. Uma's father made haste and started registering her name in all the matchmaking centers and also advertised in the newspapers, seeking a good bridegroom. Uma was depressed about the way her parents were hurrying her marriage but, however, she dare not tell them about her love affair. She kept telling her mother that she was not interested in marriage right now. But her mother only said, "All your sisters had also told the same thing in the beginning but after marriage, they hardly have time for their aged parents."

On the other hand, Ganesh's Uncle had found the details of Uma appropriate for Ganesh. Immediately, he noted down the address and came to Uma's house. On seeing the girl, he was pleased with her and took all efforts in settling this marriage. Uma had not told her mother about her missing periods and this was what made her panicky ! She hated everyone around. She became sulky and never spoke to anyone. Even without saying goodbye to her parents, she followed Ganesh to his house. And Ganesh was the poor victim of all her pent up emotions.

A month had passed after her marriage. She started appreciating Ganesh for his gentleman behaviour. The world never doubted about them and believed them to be a good husband and wife. But inside, Uma was taking her own sweet time to decide on her life, the freedom, given by Ganesh. Now, she realized that it was high time that she decided about her life. There was no point in leading a life without any rhyme or reason to her existence. She prayed to God to help her out from this tragedy. Suddenly, she remembered something and was filled with a surge of hope. The time to resolve her life was nearing after all. After Ganesh left for office, she ran to the nearby telephone booth and dialed Arathi's number.

At the time of leaving, Kumar had promised Arathi that he would send the balance rent payment within a month. Although, being a close friend, Arathi was not aware of the developments in Uma's life. When her friend came on the line, she asked her if Kumar had sent her the promised cheque. Arathi told her that she had received the payment just two days back. Uma then requested her to read out the address on the cover. Arathi rummaged her drawer for the envelope and on finding it, she read out the address to her.

After noting down the address, she thanked Arathi profusely. On reaching home, she took out a paper and pen and began writing to Kumar. Since, Ganesh had promised to abide by her decision, a divorce would not be difficult at all and thus she avoided the news of her marriage in the letter. She wished to know about the steps he was taking for their marriage and also revealed the fact that she was carrying his baby and requested that he rush her a reply advising the future course of action.

Uma waited at the doorstep anxiously for his reply, everyday. She would return dejected, after the postman passed by her house without handing over any letter. But one fine day, she received an airmail envelope. On seeing the address, her confidence bolstered and she tore open the letter in a haste and started reading it. Kumar had written :

I am really shocked to read your letter, but very much helpless right now. Here, there is plenty of opportunity for one's carrier growth and I wish to utilize the same to my utmost. This leaves me with no time for marriage and family. I just can't think of a committed life for at least another five years and it would indeed be very wise of you to get married to someone else, instead of waiting for me. As for the baby, please abort it immediately.

She felt very humiliated on reading the letter and tore it into shreds. How easily had he skydived off from responsibility. God had indeed punished her enough, for giving into temptation. Though she was aware of the consequences of getting involved with a man and had read and heard pathetic stories of how women suffered by men who had abandoned them, she was for a second, unable to listen to the rules of her mind and had listened to her heart. No one was going to find fault with Kumar because he is a man. How easily, he had asked her to abort the baby, without being aware of the physical pains she had to undergo. She cursed herself for behaving in such a manner. She was now the helpless victim of a fraud. That day, when Ganesh returned from office, Uma told him that she wished to go and stay with her parents for a while. Ganesh asked her, if he had to accompany her too, but Uma preferred to go all alone. Next day, instead of going to her parents' place, she went to the nearby hospital, and got herself admitted for an abortion. After two days, she returned home. Well ! The final curtain had at last descended in her life. Her mind was cleared of all the confusions. She had been duped by God for no fault of hers. All that was her fault was, that she had got carried away by the soft and kind words of Kumar.

During her one month stay with Ganesh, she realized that he was a kind man who cared for the feelings of others. Such a man should not be deceived and so she decided to divulge the truth to him. She was prepared to face the storm. If Ganesh was willing to accept her for what she was, she would start a new life with him and on the other hand, if he refused, she would leave him peacefully. At least, then she would be satisfied that she had not betrayed him in any manner.

That evening, when Ganesh returned home, he was in for a surprise. The lamps in the puja room were brightly lit and the fragrance of agarbatti wafted across in the air. Uma was wearing her wedding saree and on seeing him, she said, "Today, I am going to decide about my life. However, it fully depends on your decision after listening to my confession." She led him to the puja room and narrated the whole story of her life, without skipping a point. While Ganesh sat there dismayed, she concluded, "Now it is your turn to decide about your life. As for me, I am prepared for anything ! If you can't accept me for what I am, you can very well divorce me. On the other hand, if you so desire, we can begin our life afresh ! Now, the ball is in your court !"

Ganesh was sitting silently without commenting anything. Though Uma had told him, that she was prepared to accept his decision, whatever it be ; his silence filled her with tension. She felt the heavy pounding of her heart and her fingers began to tremble.

Ganesh was an invincible and optimistic man ; one, who was prepared to take the good with gratitude and the bad without self-pity, as they chanced to come his way. Clearing his throat, he slowly got up and began, "I was never given an opportunity in this life to take a decision. From a very young age, I have learnt to accept my fate that I was destined to. Like others, I never had big dreams or goals set for my life, and I grew up with a feeling that God has his own plans for me ! I have learnt to resign to my fate. I have also grown up the hard way and I somehow can feel the pangs of suffering undergone by others and always make it a point to ease the sufferings of others, in whatever possible way I can. And if I can ease your sufferings and make you feel happy in any manner, I would be willing to accept you wholeheartedly. Our scriptures are full of advice for us not to entertain the sense of doer ship in doing good as well as for bad deeds. If you wish to forget the past, and start life afresh with me, I am willing to readily accept you as my wife, without regrets."

Uma felt genuinely honoured by Ganesh. She was rather moved by his touching words. Unable to control herself, she fell down flat on to his feet. Very soon, Ganesh felt his feet turn wet. He remained standing there, letting her cry her grief away for he knew, crying on a loved ones, soothes the mind and he wished to give her that comfort so that they can start a new life after that.

2

Grandma's Advice

Ramya was getting restive as her Wedding Day was fast approaching. She had taken a month's leave from her office for the Wedding. Her mind was always pondering over Ramu her would-be husband. She kept wondering as to what type of man he would turn out to be. She was aware of the fact that it was in the hands of a woman to make a beast or an angel out of her husband.

At last, the D-day arrived and the marriage went off very well. Ramya tried her best to be very meticulous and also took all out efforts to please both her husband and mother-in-law. They went to Yercaud for their honeymoon and returned after a week. While unpacking her bags, Ramya was amazed at the fact as to how her wedding holidays had passed off so quickly. Both of them were reluctant to go to the office on Monday morning and wished to be together always. Ramya realized that life after marriage was really nice and thrilling. Also, it was a great pleasure to have someone, to whom you could reveal all the feelings.

But her happiness was short-lived. Once they started to go to office, things changed. Ramya was not able to balance the tensions of both home and workplace. She was finding it difficult to satisfy her husband at nights and also please her mother-in-law by doing all household chores. Also, she had very less time left for taking care of her own health and beauty. And even during the weekends, she was too busy. She would slog from morning till noon, washing up all her clothes, that had accumulated during the whole week.

She remembered, how just a few months back, her weekends were joyous time, when all she had to do was sleep, watch TV or read her favourite books. Life was becoming burdensome day after day and she felt the joys she experienced in the beginning of her married life were slowly descending. Also, she has come to learn the fact that her husband was a man who wanted perfection in everything and she wondered whether she would be able to please him all her life. Her efforts to be a perfectionist in everything, was telling upon her health. More so, from the time the doctor told her that she was pregnant, her health was deteriorating and she got into frequent tiffs with Ramu by not being able to meet the high standards that he desired.

One evening, as soon as Ramya reached home, she felt a bout of giddiness. She went and lay down on the bed to have a little rest. Whenever, she complained about giddiness, Ramu would become rather irked. Thus, on hearing the squeal of the brakes, she understood, that Ramu was back home. She made efforts to get up, but found everything swirling around her and so continued to there. As soon as Ramu entered the room, he was annoyed to see Ramya reclining on the bed. He had a severe headache and requested her to prepare some hot coffee. Ramya, though heard him say that, was unable to get up and move to the kitchen as her giddiness, still persisted. When he found her still lying, without stirring, Ramu became wild and shouted, "Are you going to give me coffee or not, my head is pounding?" Holding her swirling head, she went inside the kitchen, wondering how a man could be so heartless. Did he not care for her and his baby ? Her anger rose at the thought of being a wife of such a ruthless fellow. She cluttered the vessels noisily expressing her resentment and at last handed over the coffee to him. Ramu just took a long sip and remarked, "the decoction is light, the coffee is cold and has black particles floating over ; you have done this purposefully, no ?" He flung the glass on the floor. "Don't imagine that you are the only woman on earth who is pregnant", he screamed. "I have seen many pregnant woman, who are dynamic and lively all the time. If you can't carry the baby, better abort it. Don't keep grumbling all the time; I am fed up of listening to your complaints, everyday."

On hearing the sharp words, his mother intervened, "Ramu, don't you talk like that to her. A child is God's gift to us. You know how many people are weeping daily for a child ? They are spending their whole earnings for this very cause and you really don't realize the importance of it, because you have been blessed too soon. After all, getting something after great suffering, holds much significance." Ramu did not speak anything and silently left the house in a huff. When he returned, it was almost 10 p.m., and he found

Ramya deep asleep. His mother told him that she did not have her dinner as she did not feel like eating anything. Ramu did not reply to her but meekly went in to the kitchen. He opened the fridge and took out two large oranges. After preparing fresh juice out of it, he woke up Ramya. Ramya emptied the whole glass voraciously. He then begged her to forgive him for his harsh behaviour.

Of late, Ramya could not understand his character. One moment, he was yelling at her like a dog, and the next moment, he would come and talk to her as though nothing had happened. But Ramya could not forget the wound that he had caused and she would continue to be sulky and never reply to him. This would further infuriate him and result in another clash. These petty quarrels were getting very frequent. She realised that Ramu was a nitpicking husband and day after day, life with him was getting difficult.

The next day was even worse for Ramya. Her giddiness was much severe and she felt very exhausted and weak. She decided to stay back at home. In the evening, just before the return of Ramu, she got up from bed and groomed herself. There was rice to be ground and slowly she put the rice into the grinder and flicked on the switch. Once, the job was over, she felt a bit dizzy and went to the bed to lie down for a while, leaving the grinder un cleaned. Just then, Ramu returned from office and was enraged on seeing the unwashed grinder, with mosquitoes swarming around it. "I don't know what the ladies in this house are really doing," he screamed. Ramya lay on the bed silently without retorting for she knew that any thing that she uttered would provoke him further.

Just the previous week, Ramya had requested him to buy a washing machine. She told him that much time was wasted during the weekends, washing clothes and a washing machine would save a lot of time. Ramu considered her request for this meant that his wife would spend more time with him and so he quickly consented to her request. But on seeing how the grinder was left uncared for, he changed his mind. Entering the room, he yelled at Ramya, "Forget the idea of purchasing a washing machine. I could rather invest the money for some better use in the future." Ramya could not answer him. But she lay quietly wondering why he never tried to understand her sufferings and pain and spoke like a beast with no heart. Slowly, she began walking towards the kitchen to clean up the mess. Just then, her MIL entered and started bawling at Ramu, "What the hell you know about pregnant woman and agonies of morning sickness ? Why do you keep carping at her for each and everything ?"

"Your daughter-in-law imagines herself as the only pregnant woman on earth and makes a great fuss and you are dancing to her tunes," he yelled. Ramu's comparison of her with other women very often, only rubbed sand on her sour. She burst out sobbing. Hearing her sniffles, her MIL said, "Ramya is too weak and the doctor had advised her to take complete rest for one month. I have asked her to go to her parents' home for a while and I am taking her there tomorrow morning."

It was almost a week after Ramya had come to stay with her parents. She was getting a bit paranoid because Ramu had not bothered to phone up to her even once. She did not tell anything about the fight she had with him or the fact that she had come away without seeking his permission, to her mother as this would make her worried. She was harried by the fact whether this was the end of her married life and would Ramu ever come to take her home. But then, she thought that this was not the right time for a perplexed mind, for this would certainly affect the baby. She was determined to forget everything and give top priority to her baby.

The following week, her turbulent mind slackened a little, with the arrival of her grandmother from the village. On seeing Ramya, she expressed her happiness that she was going to be a great grandmother very soon. Within two days, granny noticed the transformation in the behaviour of Ramya. She was not the lively type of girl that she used to be before marriage. Grandmother decided to have a talk with her. Several times, Ramya had sought advice from grandma, whenever she had faced crisis in life. She decided to open out her heart. "Grandma, my husband is a man of perfection and expects the same from me in each and everything I do. If I fail to do it, he keeps nagging me and of late, I am unable to tolerate his nitpickings. Now that I am pregnant, I am finding it very difficult to even keep myself fit all the time and this leaves him even more angry and everyday, a quarrel breaks out between us. After shouting at me, he leaves the house in anger and after a while returns and speaks to me kindly as though nothing has happened. But how can I ever forget the wound he had inflicted upon me. My silence provokes him further and he starts blasting at me once again. I am getting fed up of this life. I just can't be a loving wife, good DIL and a housekeeper and also go out to work. I am not a Robot to be able to do all the jobs simultaneously, and nor can I be bereft of any emotions." Her grandmother listened to her complaints patiently and then said, "Ramya, avoid anger in the first place, especially now, that you are pregnant. Keep yourself cool and calm. Your anger will only affect the baby and so stop thinking of anything else but your baby, who should be your first choice right now. No marriage is without quarrels and bickering. That too, in the initial stages, these would be very frequent. This is the period when both husband and wife get to know each other well. A sought of understanding is reached between them and once this is achieved, then one can easily tackle the problems in a marriage. As you know that your husband is a nagging and nitpicking man, you can very well adjust your life to suit his taste and be free from problems. All this is part of life. You should learn to adjust with the hardships of life - only then you will find true happiness."

Ramya sat listening to her grandma very quietly and then blurted, "It is easy to preach, but very difficult to follow in life. No girl can adjust with a man like Ramu, who keeps picking at each and everything and starts up a fresh row every time. He has put me in a state of mental agony....".

Grandma was quick to interrupt, "Listen to me fully dear and then speak on. I am not preaching but telling some thing, which if you follow sincerely, would bring you all the happiness in life. We do had our fighting bouts in our life time too, but never did the idea of running away from each other occur to us even once, like you modern couples often do. I had no formal education, and in our family, husband was considered God and so we had to heed to whatever he told us to do." Ramya cut in, "But I am educated and independent.

I too have got tensions like he has and I cannot give into whatever he says."

Grandma continued, "Protest you can, my child ; but do it gently in a nice way. Then you will be dictating terms to him., your words will be law and you will be his boss without letting him know that you are acting as his boss. Whenever he is angry and blasts at you, just shut your mouth. Don't retort. The best way to deal with an argument is to avoid it. Remember Ramya, one's words can't do any harm to you, it is only your own words and actions that will hurt you. If his words are very sharp and you can't bear to listen them, just quit the place. He will repent for the harsh words spoken later on. Later, when he is cool and in a peaceful mood, tell him about your feelings. He will surely listen patiently to whatever you say. He will definitely change! Instead, if you give tit for tat, he will only develop an aversion to you. Never let that happen, Ramya."

"So, Grandma, you too are one among the common mass with the same opinion that girls are of weaker sex. You are also telling me that I should give in to whatever my husband says - adjust to his ways and attitude."

"Who on earth says that girls are of weaker sex ? It is we, who are really strong - both in mind and body. Remember, my child, by giving in, you don't become weak. It requires a very strong mind and strong will power to listen to criticism and yet keep silent without retorting. You surpass men with weak mind who shout at the slightest provocation. Anger is only a weakness."

"But it is not easy to practise, Grandma. How can I keep my mouth shut, when he is talking bull shit? And after creating a Tornado, he would come to me and speak as though nothing has happened, forgetting the pain he had inflicted in me. Does he expect me to be a block of wood without any feelings?"

"Let me explain to you in a better way. If we strike a toddler for doing a wrong or any of the tantrums, he will only weep but would not rejoin or retaliate you. In fact, he will come back to you in a short while, forgetting the whole incident and without any grudge against you. This submissive act on the part of the child will make you feel sorry for the kid and for your brutal act. You will later caress, fondle and even plum him. Similarly, when you bear the brunt silently, you too would be rewarded by your husband in the form of implicit obedience and kindness which will come by itself in the due course. If you practise it sincerely, though hard it may seem in the beginning, it will slowly become a habit. After all, life is full of adjustments and we only gain a lot by giving in. You will then experience a unique pleasure which is peerless. Ramya, I had practised this art so well that sometimes when your Grandpa's reproaches, deafen my ears, I cannot help laughing to myself."

Ramya started to imagine, how Ramu would react, if she also laughed in front of him, while he kept railing at her and suddenly burst out laughing. Somehow, unburdening herself to her Grandma gave her some relief and her dejected mood got lighter. She was now bent upon following the advice given by her grandmother and was also determined to stop further arguments with Ramu.

Ramya's leave was coming to an end. Her Morning sickness was over and she started feeling better now.

It was Saturday and she began packing her bags to go to her in-law's house the next day. That evening, when she was watching TV, she heard the door bell chime and went to answer it. She was astonished to see Ramu standing outside and for a minute joy writ large on her face. Pulling her close to him, he said, "Enough of enjoying in your mom's house, come along with me right away. I am feeling very bored without you and our separation seems like ages to me. I have realised that life is void to me without you." Ramya wrenched herself off from his hold, before anybody could notice it and said, "I too have been feeling the same way."

He then stared at the faded and worn out saree which Ramya was wearing, that too high above her heels, and was quick to make a sarcastic comment on that. But this time, Ramya went in and returned wearing one of Ramu's favourite sarees. Ramu was glad to note the change in her and said, "I think, we can expect some rain tonight. For once, you have tried to please me without countering."Ramya kept blushing and did not retort to his comments. Grandma was watching the whole drama and her face brightened. She felt happy that the advice she had given had at last transformed her granddaughter. But for how long, only God knows !

3

The Embarrassment

Meenakshi could not bear it any longer. Everyone's eyes were on her and they were anxious about her next move. Though she had been standing there for just a minute, it seemed like ages. Suddenly, an idea struck her and she said to the small crowd hovering around her, "The scooter was running on reserve since last evening and now he had gone to the nearest petrol pump. Anyway, thanks for all your help. I will meet him on the way", and she started walking. Slowly, the people began moving. Seeing the crowd disperse, Meenakshi felt much relieved and thanked God for His timely intervention which enabled her to handle such an embarrassing situation.

Lifting the heavy bag, filled to the brim with the provisions for the month, Meenakshi somehow approached a pavement and decided to halt there. She sat down in a corner, so that she would be easily visible to her husband, and placed the bag beside her. She examined the red weal on her palms, caused by the straps of the bag. To add to that, the sun was blazing down at her and she fervently hoped that her husband returns soon, to pick her up. But at the same time her mind was clouded with doubts also. For she has reasons. She knew that the moment her husband thought of her, he was going to come back in search of her. But when was it going to be and for how long she had to wait for him in the scorching sun ?

This was not the first time. Ever since she married Rajesh, he had been a pain in her neck. He was a man with great ambition, always trying to reach for the sky. He had a lot in his mind and forgetting things was his nature. He was always filled with stress and was so much concerned about the security of the future that he did not enjoy the present life. In the beginning, Meenakshi was always on her toes, lingering around him and helping him to find the misplaced things. The mornings used to be tension-filled when he would be yelling at her for the keys, glasses, watch, pens, or the purse. And Meenakshi would obligingly run around from one place to another looking for them. As years passed by and after having two children, it became difficult for her to manage with his forgetfulness. One day, she decided to set him in the right path and told him curtly, "I just don't have enough time to keep trailing behind you finding out your things; which you carelessly misplace. After all, I have to attend the children too; so you ought to be careful and stop depending on me." And as a sequel to this outburst, she called the carpenter and got a stand erected in the hall, exclusively meant for her husband. She then ordered him to place all his paraphernalia in the three racks of the stand. The children were strictly warned not to get near the stand and meddle with daddy's things, which they complied with.

However, other things kept slipping out of his mind very often. Sometimes, on the way, when he chanced to meet one of Meenakshi's friends, he took an active part in the conversation, along with his wife, by nodding his head from time to time and also airing his opinion. After seeing her off, he turned to his wife and asked, "By the way, what was her name ?" And all that Meenakshi could do was to laugh at his stupidity. At times, he would not leave the bed at 6 a.m. which was his usual time to get up for the day, and when his wife would caution him, he would coolly say, "It is Saturday and let me enjoy my weekend". Then Meenakshi would start the usual nagging and bickering about his memory loss and remind him that it was Friday and he was getting late for his office.

Slowly, the children started poking fun on their father too. One day Meenakshi overheard their conversation, in which they were referring to their father as AMPS instead of the usual APPS, which was the short form of APPA meaning father. On seeking clarification, she learnt that the children had nicknamed their father as "Absent-Minded Professor". This, they did on the day, when he had scolded them for being very sloppy and undisciplined. It so happened that one fine day when Rajesh, settled comfortably on the sofa with a news magazine, wondered why the letters were looking so blurred. At once, he remembered that he was not wearing the glasses and started searching for the same, everywhere. Just then, the children had returned from their tuition classes, and he pounced on them like a mad dog, "why the hell are you meddling with the things in my shelf ? Who has taken my glasses ? I can't find them any where ?" The children chuckled together and said, "How can you find it, when it is resting over your head?"

But after his retirement, things began getting even worse. His memory made him a butt of fun and laughter in the family. Meenakshi had spent her whole life teasing and nagging him for his habit. But after his retirement, when he was there at home lingering around her, with nothing to do, she started to pity him. Her husband had always been a busybody and now, she felt sorry to see him idling in the early morning hours, either gaping outside the window blankly or standing by his children during breakfast advising and sharing his experience with them. Suddenly, Meenakshi's attitude towards him changed. She softened towards her husband. And now, since her children were all grown up, she viewed her husband as a child who required her wholehearted care and devotion. From a nagging and bossing type of woman, Meenakshi transformed herself into a kind and loving wife with humility; so much so that, once when her husband had forgotten to flush the toilet, she silently did the job, before the children could find out and never reproached her husband at all. And if the children ever laughed at his forgetfulness, she would admonish them and ask them to be serious in life and not laugh at other's expense. But today, things had gone a bit too far.

In the morning, Rajesh was busy watering the plants, when Meenakshi reminded him, that they had to go out to procure the provisions for the month. Rajesh finished his gardening work and went in to change his clothes. As they stepped out of the house, Meenakshi expressed her opinion, "I feel it would be much better if we take an auto". Suddenly his spirits fell and he replied, "I don't like to travel by auto, as they demand huge sums and I can't afford to squander my hard earned money". And while starting his scooter, he said proudly, "Perhaps my memory may be weak ; but I have still not forgotten to ride a scooter. I have sharp eyes and ears and I am still young at heart."

Being the first week of the month, the Supermarket was fully packed. Though Meenakshi picked up her items within half an hour, the long queue at the billing counter irked her. And when she stepped out of the air-conditioned center to the parking zone, the dazzling sun almost burnt her skin. Now, she wanted to reach home soon. She prodded her husband to start the vehicle quickly. All of a sudden, her husband remembered something, and he slapped his palm on his forehead complaining, "I had all the while been thinking to buy a medicated toothpaste for my sensitive teeth and it somehow skipped out of my mind." The ordeal of getting into that crowded shopping complex once again was unthinkable and before he could utter another word, Meenakshi advised him to purchase it from a medical shop on the way and mounting the vehicle, she comfortably sat down behind him. Consenting to her idea, he began to kick-start the scooter. Without having any response, he performed the same action with greater enthusiasm, again and again but with no success. Turning back, he requested his wife to get down and once again gave it a hard kick. But the vehicle did not budge and he felt dejected.

By now, a few passers-by gathered around them, and offered their help. However, the vehicle refused to start. Rubbing the sweat off her forehead, Meenakshi was cursing the sun. Having lost all hope, she suggested her husband to look around for a mechanic shop, when all of a sudden, a college student butted in from nowhere.

His first few attempts met with failure, then he bent his head to examine the root cause of the problem, and at last found it. The keys were dangling loosely from the slot, and the scooter was locked. He opened it and lightly kicked the vehicle and this time the engine roared. The crowd appreciated the young boy for his presence of mind.

Rajesh felt awkward ; for once again, he was a victim of memory loss. Slowly, he climbed on to the scooter. Meenakshi felt her head with the palm and exclaimed, "It really is one of the worst summers, I have ever experienced in my life." While she adjusted her saree pallu, to cover her head and was getting ready to sit down behind her husband, her husband gave a light kick and the engine revved up instantly. His face brightened and without as much as looking back, he zoomed off down the road excitedly.

On his way, he kept reveling in the fact that the young boy saved his time and money by avoiding a trip to the mechanic. However, since his memory had once again failed him, he felt rather ashamed and said, "Well, I may be an absent-minded person, but what happened to you ? You keep bragging all the time that you do not forget anything and that you look too young for your age. Why you did not point it out to me, then ? Being young also means sharpness of mind, isn't it ?" There was no reply from his wife. He was quite shocked that she was silent without retaliating. He immediately turned his head and came to an abrupt halt. "Oooh !" he blurted out. "What a messy thing have I done ? How could I ever forget my wife ?" He was vexed with himself for being so thoughtless. Turning back, he rode his scooter swiftly along the road, to pick up his wife ; well prepared for a dressing down from her.

Five minutes had gone by, and Meenakshi was losing hope that her husband would return shortly. Deciding to go by an auto, she stood up and instantly, she saw her husband. After parking his vehicle, he walked towards her sullenly. On approaching her, his face lit up with a sheepish grin and as he bent down to lift the heavy bag, he said, "In the ensuing excitement that followed the starting of our scooter, I had forgotten all about you." Meenakshi very calmly said, "When you revved up your scooter and buzzed off without me ; at first, I thought you were trial checking your vehicle. But when you had gone straight without even looking back, I knew for sure, that I should have slipped out of your mind. You must have seen the look on the faces of the people, pausing for an explanation from me. But how could I let down my husband ? Somehow, I bluffed to them that you had gone to the petrol bunk and tided over from an embarrassing situation."

4

The Beauty Queen

Kamya was looking into the mirror, one last time and giving final touches to her make-up before leaving with her husband for the wedding function. After their marriage, for the first time, she was much exulted to accompany him. The ravishing silk saree she wore, enhanced her beauty further and as she entered the marriage hall, everyone's eyes were on the couple. At the entrance, three young girls standing in front of a large table, were inviting the guests in the traditional manner by sprinkling scented water on the guests and offering sugar candies while one of them, was handing out rose flowers to the women. Kamya smiled at her, after collecting the rose and as she started to leave, she could hear the conversation the girls were having, behind her.

"Look, how beautiful that lady looks ; just like an actress."

"Yah, she is like a beauty queen."
"But look at her husband, how dark he is."
"I bet he can't be her husband."

Just then, Ravi held Kamya's hand and directed her to the empty chair nearby and as Kamya comfortably seated herself in it, she could see the look of bewilderment on their faces. But their talk had not affected Kamya at all, like it used to, in the past.

During the early days of her marriage, whenever she went out with her husband, she would hear people murmuring on how unmatched pair they were. "She is as fair and beautiful like a swan while he is a dark crow," they said. The words pained her beyond relief and fighting back her tears, she would curse her fate which had resulted in her marriage with this dark man.

Kamya was born in a middle-class family. She was the most pretty baby with lovely features and everyone in the neighbourhood vied with each other to lift her up and hold her for some time. Her father was no doubt, proud of his beautiful daughter. Though he was an ordinary clerk, who worked very hard to make both ends meet, he never closed his fists when it came to spending for his loving daughter. He would work on weekends and on holidays, foregoing his pleasures, to earn extra income so that he could bring up his daughter in a luxurious manner. He would always buy the costliest dress for her and also sent her to the best convent school in town. Very often, he would boast to his wife, "When my daughter grows up, she is going to be the most beautiful woman, ever born on this earth." On hearing these words, his wife would retort, "but don't boast so much ; for one fine day, a prince will carry off your daughter, and you will be left all alone." Growing up listening to such conversations, Kamya was naturally filled with conceit about her beautiful looks and she would start dreaming about the handsome prince.

When Kamya grew up, her father's prohecy indeed trurned out to be true. She was so attractive that people who passed by her, wished to have a second glance at her. All her friends envied her beauty and they would often tease her, "Would you like to exchange your long and lustrous hair ?" Or "Wow, you have such enchanting eyes." At home, Kamya would recount everything to her parents and make them feel elated. However, the moment of elation was only short-lived and her father would immediately start worrying about Kamya's future. Whenever he saw the rich girls getting out of their cars and entering the posh shops to do their shopping, his mind would suddenly move on to his own daughter, who could enjoy life only at the petty sacrifices he made from time to time. He always kept dreaming that, a day would come indeed and his daughter would get married into a rich family and then she will enjoy the luxuries of life, without having to calculate the expenses involved for each and everything.

When Kamya finished college, many handsome men came forward to wed her, but her father disapproved them. He told his daughter, "My dear girl, marry a man who has a lot of money. These days, without money, you can do nothing. How much I yearned to deck you with jewels and costly apparels. But by working overtime, foregoing my holidays and weekends and saving money only was I able to give you the best education and fulfil all your desires, keeping you ignorant of the difficulties I had undergone all my life.

If you marry a man who goes to a nine to five job, you would be struggling all your life trying to make both ends meet, like your dad. I want you to marry the richest man in this world." On hearing her father's advice, Kamya would wonder, what was her father up to.

One day, Murthi, Kamya's uncle had come to her house. On seeing his brother's daughter, his thoughts immediately went to Ravi, his young boss. Somehow, he felt an urgency to settle Ravi's marriage with Kamya, for his boss had no parents and who else would come forward to settle the young man's marriage. Murthi thought that after marriage his boss would forget the past sorrows, which still engulfed him and he would have some one to lean on and vent out his grief. Murthi discussed it with his brother and also took him to Chennai to see the boy and settle the marriage at once, for he believed that auspicious functions are not to be delayed for any reason.

On seeing the colossal bungalow, car and the servants running after Ravi, Kamya's father was so much impressed that he decided then and there, to wed his daughter to this young man. He did not worry about the conduct of the boy, as his brother assured him of that. Somehow, he had a feeling that Kamya could lead a happy and carefree life by marrying Ravi and so he had invited the boy to his house. But things had not turned out, as he desired, for when Kamya saw the boy, she did not like him, just because he was of dark complexion. She had all the while been imagining to marry a tall, fair and attractive hero. When she told this to her father, he advised her, "If you marry this man, I am sure, you will be happy all your life and you will get all the love from him. Moreover, his was a story from rags to riches and hence has come up the social ladder, the hard way and so he can understand the feelings of others. He is now starving for love and has got all the money in the world. If only you consider it over and change your mind, your future will be bright as a star."

But Kamya was adamant. After brooding over it for a considerable time, she told her father, "He may be a rich man, father ; but he is simply not the man, I had been dreaming all the while. Money alone is not the main source of happiness. While money can indeed buy all the materialistic pleasures, it certainly cannot buy the peace of mind and happiness."

Seeing that Kamya was not interested in this alliance, her father silently dropped the matter. Though he had promised Ravi that he would get back to him, in a week's time, he decided to remain silent without giving any negative reply to him.

It was a period of recession and all around, the business activity was dwindling day after day. The economic situation was also going from bad to worse and in every organisation, the voluntary retirement schemes was the watchword. One fine day, Kamya was watching a thrilling movie in the TV, when all of a sudden, she saw her father return from office. He was in a very gloomy mood and never even greeted his daughter with his usual loving smile. Kamya wondered if anything was wrong with him. Switching off the TV, she followed him and asked him why he looked so grumpy and depressed. It was only then, that her father informed her that he had opted for the voluntary retirement scheme. He explained that if he did not retire now voluntarily, then he may have to undergo much hardships in the form of transfers to distant places or even be forced to accept retirement with a lesser package than that what was offered right now.

He deposited his money in a bank and maintained the family with the interests he earned out of it. Now that his fists were tightly closed, he started feeling the pinch of money. Once again the thoughts of Ravi came to his mind and one evening, he called his daughter and brought up the subject to her. "Since your father is jobless and the few lakhs which I got as settlement for my services, will suffice only for a short time to eke out our day to day life, I am afraid, whether I will be able to ever find a suitable bridegroom for you. If you marry Ravi, you will enjoy a carefree life instead of slogging over a job or waiting for your husband's salary every month. If you obey your dad, your life will take a swift change for the best."

Kamya realised that each time, her father only kept elaborating on the positive aspects of marrying Ravi and never did he once, force her to marry him. She reflected that unlike other fathers, who don't consider their daughters' opinion, and coax them into marrying the man they choose, her father had been almost pleading with her. Suddenly, her heart melted and she started feeling pity towards the old man. And just to please her father, she reluctantly agreed to wed Ravi. While she had made her parents happy, she had destroyed her own life.

From the very first day, Ravi could make out that something was bothering Kamya. Though he did not ask her, he could sense that she was very unhappy over the marriage and that it was a forced one. During the first few months, when Ravi had taken her out to the parties, Kamya had silently followed him. She found that everyone were craning their necks to have a second look at them and stared at her, wondering if something was wrong with this girl. She would hear the petty comments they were making behind her, and on returning home, she would cry all alone for having been fated to wed a man whom she did not love. Then slowly, an idea came to her mind. If you can't change a situation, the best possible thing is to adapt to the situation, by trying to change yourself. And so she decided to change her own life and stay indoors and not go out with her husband anywhere. She preferred to keep herself busy by watching TV or reading novels etc. Whenever Ravi requested her to join him for a party, she would avoid, on one pretext or the other. Finally, Ravi decided not to disturb her anymore and started going out alone.

One Sunday evening, a friend of hers, who had also moved to Chennai after her marriage dropped at her place. She invited her for the *Vaddai Kappu*, a function which marks the celebration of the eighth month of pregnancy and Kamya readily agreed to attend the function. On that day, she also met Kamya's husband at the entrance and invited him also for the function and Ravi readily agreed.

On the day of the function, Kamya woke up early and got dressed quickly. The opening and shutting of the wardrobes awoke Ravi and on seeing that his wife was already attired for the function, he sat up on the bed. Before he could utter anything, Kamya spoke up, "Well, I did not like to disturb your sleep ; since you had come home very late last night. I shall attend the function all alone and you may continue your sleep." Ravi wondered, why she was hurrying so much, though the function was scheduled only at 9 a.m. He then asked her, "Shall I ask the driver to pick you up ?" Kamya was relieved at last that her husband had decided not to accompany her after all. Though she very much wanted to go in the car, waiting for the driver might take some time, and she feared that her husband would change his mind in the meanwhile and would be willing to attend the function along with her and so hurriedly she blurted, "I am planning to drive the Kinetic Honda myself, as my friend's house is quite nearby and I don't need the driver." Scurrying down the steps, she remembered the words her father had told her while teaching her to drive the vehicle - "You might find it useful one day." She gave out a long sigh, as she started the scooter, for little did she think that her father's lessons might be useful to her in this manner - for running away from the man, she did not love.

Though it was only 8 a.m. in the morning, the sun was blazing down at her. For the past six months, she was confined to only air-conditioned room and cars and being in the sun made her uncomfortable. The traffic was too heavy too and unmindful of the following traffic behind her or at her sides, she blindly kept following a car that was speeding across in front of her. At one particular spot, the car driver applied a sudden break and Kamya ran into the rear of the car, and was ultimately thrown off the vehicle. Kamya was attempting to get up, but as the vehicles kept moving in quick succession one after another, she was immediately hit by a motorbike, which almost smashed her right leg and she fell off balance. Suddenly, she experienced a sharp cutting pain in her right leg. She was helped by the traffic policeman, who took her to the nearby hospital. Her knee was bleeding profusely and her leg was swelling up like a balloon. Even a slightest movement caused acute pain and Kamya was crying aloud, due to the unbearable pain.

Ravi was just getting ready for breakfast, when the phone rang. He ran to pick it up. On hearing about the accident, he was almost shocked and immediately dashed to the hospital. The acute pain had exhausted her. The nurse had give her a pain killer injection. Though it was of very little help, Kamya felt her head swirling around and ultimately fell unconscious. When Ravi saw her in this state, tears welled up in his eyes. Her leg was almost a pulp and for a moment, a wild thought, as to whether his wife could walk perfectly once agin, crossed his mind. The doctor after examining her, told him that an immediate surgery had to be performed. While the operation was going on, Ravi informed her parents about the accident.

It was late in the evening, when Kamya came back to consciousness and as she opened her eyes, she saw her husband and her parents waiting in the room. On seeing her leg, which was enveloped with huge metal cases and plasters, the tears flowed in her eyes. Ravi kept assuring her that things will get better very soon and that she could walk like before.

One month had passed by and Kamya was feeling uneasy to be tied up to the bed. She very much longed to run around freely. In the evenings, Ravi visited her and spent his time with her. Though he spoke affectionately with her, little did he know that his comforting and assuring words, were only rubbing sand on her wound, for Kamya had not learnt her lesson even now. She resented his coming and the hatred she had for her husband had increased further. For, Kamya kept cursing her fate, that had her husband been handsome and fair, she would have gone out with him and would have not met with such an accident. But there was no use crying over spilled milk and so whenever she saw her husband, the hatred returned and she silently cursed him for being partly responsible for her present condition.

On the other hand, Ravi loved her very much and like a mother who tolerates the tantrums of her son, he put up with all the sufferings and pains inflicted by her from time to time. On the day of the function when she drove the Kinetic Honda by herself, though he tried to sleep, he could not and kept panicking all the while, if she would reach the destination safely. He ran down the steps after her, wishing to tell her to go by an auto, but she had already sped. Ravi had been waiting for her return when all of a sudden the phone rang and he hastened to pick it up with a premonition of hearing some bad news which, in fact, turned out to be true. He dashed to the hospital at once, skipping his breakfast. The drive to the hospital seemed to be an endless journey of destructive emotions and thoughts.

Ravi was born in a peasant family. Unlike other parents in the village, his parents wished to educate him. Though they depended on the meagre salary the landlord cared to pay them from time to time, they somehow managed to send their son to a school in a city. They never liked their son to toil in the hot fields like they did and dreamt that one day, he would become a big officer. Ravi studied so hard and his one aim in life was to make money, to buy a big mansion, to bring his parents to the city and then provide them all the luxuries of life. Ravi was lucky enough for he succeeded in achieving all his goals, one after another, by dint of hard work. One fine day, he went to his home town and asked his parents to move along with him, as he had now purchased his own bungalow. His parents requested him for some time, as they had to dispose off their property, and also settle their dues. Giving them sufficient funds, for the settlement, Ravi told them to move to his new house at the earliest. On the day of their arrival, Ravi had gone to the railway station to receive them. But when the train arrived, his parents were not to be seen. Ravi was getting impatient. His eyes were scanning around for his old parents, but they were nowhere in the vicinity. He started looking for them and as he walked on, he saw a small crowd at the opposite side of the railway track. Curious, he went to find out what had happened. And what he saw, shocked him beyond relief and he swooned.

Ravi's parents, after getting down from the train, started looking around for their son. Not finding him on the platform, they slowly began walking, searching for him. Then finally, their eyes fell on Ravi, who was also searching for his parents on the opposite platform, separated by a railway track. Since, their voice was not audible to him, they decided to cross the track, instead of using the foot over bridge. In their excitement, they were crossing the lonely track, when all of a sudden, a local suburban train ran over them, and their bodies got smashed and a small crowd had gathered there.

After his parents passed away, Ravi developed a hatred to life in general. He cursed god and wondered whether it was for this end that God had been kind to him and fulfilled his wish and made him a heavy weight businessman. He wanted to show his parents the luxurious life he was leading but unfortunatley, they had left him too soon. From then on, money meant nothing to Ravi. He simply worked because immersing himself in work gave him sound satisfaction. And money kept pouring in. His company raised in reputation and the profits kept increasing year after year.

It took almost two years for Ravi to come out of the shock and moaning. The money he made from his business, was distributed mostly in charity, helping the needy. His servants enjoyed in his house and all his employees grew rich because of his hard work. It was during this time that, Murthi, his subordinate and well-wisher, introduced him to Kamya's father, for he knew that having brought up his daughter in a very rich atmosphere, his brother was now searching for an affluent bridegroom to wed her.

Ravi too felt that life was meaningless, unless you have someone who is loving and caring, to whom, you could vent out your feelings and emotions. And so, when Murthi compelled him to get married, he readily agreed. But unfortunately, just a few days after his marriage, he realised that Kamya disliked this marriage. From her truculent behaviour, he could easily read between the lines that she was not interested in him.

Inspite of her abhorrence towards him, he continued to love her. He appreciated her for marrying him, despite her unwillingness, just to please her father. He thought that since God had gifted her with divine beauty, it was appropriate on her part to be proud and haughty. He adored her for her sacrificing nature. Somehow, being an optimistic person, Ravi believed that, time assuages everything, and one day, Kamya would start loving him. There was no point in leading a purposeless life, where you don't have anyone to love you or you don't have anyone to express your love. And so, now, Ravi felt happy that at least he had Kamya, whom he could love in spite of her insolence and waited patiently for that moment, when she would become a little subdued.

The D-day had at last arrived and Kamya was excited that she could walk, once again, after being tied up to the bed for so long. She was anxiously waiting for the doctor. But things did not turn out as she had anticipated. After the doctor gingerly removed the plaster of her leg, he asked her to walk around a few steps. When Kamya did so, she felt the same surging pain and after hobbling a few steps, immediately sat down on the bed, crying that she was not able to even stand. The doctor was himself dumbfounded and did not know, what was exactly wrong with her. He left the room silently and Kamya's mother followed him nervously.

When she returned, Kamya understood from her expression that bad news was in-store for her. Her mother informed her, "Doctor says that another major surgery has to be performed and the money involved will be running into several lakhs."

It was at that particular moment that Kamya's mind was gripped with fear. Cold sweat broke out on her forehead. She was confident that her husband would take care of the money part. But what if this operation too proves to be a failure. Would she have to remain a cripple all her life, walking with crutches? How rightly has it been said that Pride comes before a fall and now she was a victim of her vanity and bragging.

The evening was turning into twilight and with the darkness, the fear in Kamya's mind kept assenting every second. Now, she waited eagerly for Ravi and as he entered the room, she saw him in a different light. The pride of her beauty had all gone. Ravi was no longer the ugly fellow, whom she detested to see. All of a sudden, he acquired a special significance, and she looked upon him as a Saviour. As usual, Ravi sat down beside her, on the edge of the bed. Immediately, Kamya grabbed both his hands, and burying her face into them wept like a small child. Ravi who was much disturbed by her sobs, tried to stop her from getting very emotional and enquired from her mother, as to what was wrong with her. She explained everything to him. Ravi held Kamya's shoulders from rocking and spoke gently, "Please calm down dear ! Don't lose your heart ; you are going to walk again, very soon. Tomorrow, I shall consult the best doctors in the city for their expert advice, before going in for another operation. And if required, I don't mind shelling out all my wealth to see you walk again. And this is a promise !"

And Ravi had indeed fulfilled his promise. This time, as the doctor threw away the metal case and bandages telling her that it was not required anymore, Kamya too cast off her pride and vanity of her beauty, which had almost destroyed her life. She could not express her happiness in words. Slowly, she walked up to her husband and hugging him close, said, "I love you, dear." Ravi had not been waiting in vain after all. This was the transformation, for which, he had been waiting patiently. Kamya had learnt it the hard way that love triumphs everything. No more did the comments or opinions of others matter to her. She realised that beauty unlike love would get withered with age but her husband's love for her would be everlasting.

5

Another Love Story

Kamala heard the alarm clock shrill. She turned over, switched it off and continued to sleep. She was nearing Sixty and was bed-ridden most of the time. Her body ache was too much unbearable of late, and she felt comfortable lying in bed, rather than moving around. But fifteen years ago, things had been quite different. On hearing the sound of the alarm, Kamala would jump out of her bed, and run to the bathroom with her toothbrush. After finishing her bath, puja and cooking, which were her daily routine, she would begin her home business.

When Kamala was hardly thirty- five years old, her husband passed away and she was burdened with the responsibility of taking care of her two children. Not knowing what to do, she knocked at the door of her close relatives, but they only turned her down. That was when an idea struck her. She remembered that her husband often appreciated her cooking. She was an ace in preparing sweets, snacks and pickles. She decided to turn her ability into a fortune. She began her home business of making papads, pickles, sweets and snacks and started distributing it to various shops in her town. Slowly, money flowed in and she began engaging two other woman who also assisted her in her work. She then became confident of maintaining the family single-handedly. She admitted her two children into a good school. The children too, realized the hard work their mother was doing, and worked very hard and passed their exams with high marks. When her daughter finished graduation, Kamala fixed her marriage immediately and felt so relieved as one part of her responsibility was now over. Now, it was her son who was the cause for her worry all the time. Whenever the subject of marriage was brought up, he would get wild and begin to yell at her, "I need some time to settle down in life. Don't force me into a committed life now. Until my ambitions are fulfilled, I can't get married." Fed up of the same reply, whenever the subject of marriage was mooted, Kamala at last, decided to give up.

Kamala was in a deep slumber, when she heard the tap on the door. At last she woke up and she was shocked that the sun had already risen and Gopal was just getting ready to his office. She ran into the kitchen and started making idlies, skipping her usual routine of bath and puja. She was almost done with her job and was packing her son's tiffin box, when she heard the sound of his motorbike. She knew that Gopal was very particular about punctuality and would leave by sharp 9 a.m. every day. Many a times, Gopal had told her not to bother about him. He had a canteen in his office and he could take his lunch there but Kamala would never allow him to take any outside food as she believed that they were unhygienic and could lead to some health hazards.

Bawling aloud for him to stop for a while, she started running towards the door, when all of a sudden, she slipped on the doormat and fell down. Hearing the thud, Gopal parked his vehicle and came in. Seeing his mother struggle to get up, he helped her to the nearby sofa. Handing over the pain balm to her he yelled, "how many times have I told you not to bother about my lunch box ? Why don't you listen to what I say ?" Kamala had heard it umpteen times and she would just remain silent, without retorting. But today, the pain in her leg was unbearable and she decided to give vent to her feelings, "Do you listen to whatever I say ? Have I not told you time and again to get married and settle in life. I would then be free from housework and take rest. Can't you see that I am getting old, day after day. All my life, I had never woken up so late and skipped my routine. Don't you have any kind feelings towards your mother? I too need to retire in life and play with my grandchildren, but that can happen only when you get married." Gopal remained silent. His silence further provoked her and she said, "May be I am destined to slog all my life, and I don't know when God is going to be kind to me."

In the evening, when Gopal returned home, he saw his mother lying in bed in a disheveled manner. He was worried as he had never seen his mother lying down like this. Slowly, he went inside and switched on the light in her room. Sitting beside her, he said, "Well, mother, you can start seeing a girl for me. I am now ready for marriage. Now that I have completed my MBA, the much-awaited promotion is in the offing. Marriage would have been an hindrance to both my studies and job and that is why, I had been postponing it all the time." Even before Gopal finished his talk, Kamala slowly tried to get out of the bed. God alone knows where the pain had disappeared. On hearing this she walked up to the bathroom all by herself and after refreshing herself, started for the temple to thank God, for her son had at last agreed for marriage.

In the temple, while the pujari was offering her prasad, she informed him that she wished to have a talk with him. Within a few minutes, the crowd gathered there trailed off and the pujari meekly walked up to her and sat down beside her. Kamala took out her son's horoscope from her purse and handing it over to him said, "Today is a lucky day in my life. My son has agreed for his marriage and now the responsibility of finding a good bride for him lies with you." The pujari examined the horoscope for a long time. Then slowly, he took out a folded sheet of paper from his pocket and started comparing it with the horoscope.

Two months back, a close friend of his, had given this to him and pleaded that he somehow find a suitable match for his daughter. As he studied the two horoscopes, his face brightened. Settling marriages was a job he enjoyed most and it also brought him some extra revenue every month. He was well known by the people in the neighbourhood as marriage broker who fixed the marriages within a short duration. But this particular girl's horoscope was lying with him for nearly two months and only a few days back, he placed it at the feet of Lord and requested Him for his blessings. Now, he was happy that the horoscopes matched well and immediately he scribbled out the address of the girl and gave it to Kamala and said, "There is a very good match for your son. This Sunday, I shall take you to the girl's house. Also inform your son to keep himself free for the girl-seeing function. In the meanwhile, I shall apprise the girl's parents to be ready to receive you." Kamala was very much thrilled. At last, she was going to have a daughter-in-law. She would then be relieved of household chores and could spend her time happily with her grandchildren, till the end of her life. Though there was still a mild pain in her leg, she walked faster to convey the good news to her son.

Ramani was fair and beautiful. When Gopal saw the girl, he liked her, the very instant. Kamala too was satisfied with the bride to be and she turned around and enquired her son in a hushed tone, if he liked her. She got a positive response from him and so continued her conversation with the girl's parents. When the topic turned to dowry, Gopal became restless. He wished to run away from there but since he had no other go, he continued sitting there, peeking into the newspaper.

For Kamala, money had been one of the obsessions all her life. After her husband's death she had learned it the hard way, that without money, no one respected you. None of her relatives helped them. That was when she lost the love for people and embarked upon earning money. By slogging over day in and day out, she achieved her goal. After that there was a constant flow of money, and she educated her children very well, purchased a house and also conducted the marriage of her daughter.

Since she got her daughter married into a rich family, she had spent all her savings of a lifetime. But she had no regrets, for it was her own daughter. Further, she had confidence that she could earn the money within a few years. But things did not go as per her plan. Immediately after her daughter's marriage, she developed arthiritis and back ache. The pain was so acute that every night when she lay down in the bed, she kept moaning for a long time, until sleep came to her. When Gopal came to know about this he told his mother firmly, "Stop doing your business from tomorrow. Now that I have got a good job, I shall take care of you. All you have to do is, just cook for the two of us." The next day, he paid up the dues to the two women who worked for his mother and sent them home. Thus her home business came to an abrupt end.

From then on, Kamala spent her time cooking, watching television and in the nearby temple. But her mind was constantly regretting the fact that, had she been healthy, she could have left behind a huge saving for her son and his children. Now, when she learnt that Ramani was the only daughter, her greed was aroused. She decided to utilize this opportunity to bring in some wealth into the family, and decided to demand a huge dowry. According to her, she would be indirectly helping her son.

Turning to Ramani's parents she said,"I am interested in going ahead with this marriage. As you know my son is now working in a Multinational Company as a Manager. There were very good offers from affluent families who were prepared to send their daughters with more than a hundred sovereigns of gold. But Gopal had been refusing to marry all the while, under one pretext or the other and only now he has given his consent for the marriage. I am sure that being your only child, you would not send your daughter decked with less than a fifty sovereigns of gold jewels. The moment you let me know of your willingness, we shall fix up the wedding date and commence the arrangement for the same."

Ramani's father liked the boy. His inner conscience told him that his loving daughter would be able to lead a happy life with this boy, for he climbed up the social ladder, the hard-way. He also learnt that Gopal was an obedient son to his mother, who brought up him in a well-disciplined manner. Ramani's father was working in an government organization and had hardly a year for retirement. With his savings, he was just able to buy thirty sovereigns of jewels for his daughter's marriage. Adding his wife's jewels also, there would be just another ten sovereigns. Now he wondered, where would he be able to get the remaining ten sovereigns. He then considered having another meeting with the boy's mother so as to bargain with her and change her mind regarding the fifty sovereigns, but later gave up the idea. For he reasoned, that if he got his daughter married with only forty sovereigns, she would become a victim of her mother-in-law who would be pricking and nagging her all the time. After racking his brains for almost a week, he finally decided to drop this alliance.

Gopal waited patiently for a response from the bride's family. When it was almost a month, he became restless. His mother too, who was all the while pressurizing him in this matter, remained silent. He wished to know about the progress, but felt rather shy to ask his mother. He did not wish to express his eagerness, for she would chide him for pretending to be disinterested in marriage all these years. One fine day, after office hours, he went to the temple and met the pujari to get the information. "Did your mother not tell you anything ?", the pujari exclaimed. "The girl's father told me that he could not afford fifty sovereigns as dowry. When I conveyed this to your mother, she bluntly told me that she was not interested in this alliance and asked me to see some other girl for you. In fact, I am planning to meet her with another girl's address, shortly." Gopal was boiling inside. Was his mother so heartless, he wondered !. He was very furious. Did she consider him to be a doll, without any emotions ? Did she ever bother to discuss the matter with him ? When it comes to settling the marriages of their sons, all mothers become avaricious and he realized that his mother was not an exception.

Ramani's innocent face, kept darting in front of him very often and he could not erase her from his mind, for he had already fallen in love with her, but at the same time, he did not like to hurt his mother and do anything against her will. He believed in God and had confidence that whatever He does will be the best and cleared his mind to let fate take its own course!

One evening, Gopal returned from office in a very excited mood. He had passed his MBA exam in first class and his boss had also handed over his promotion letter to him. He gave the promotion letter to his mother and asked her to bless him. Kamala was bouncing with happiness the whole day. When her son gave her the promotion letter, her happiness was doubled. Immediately, she ran in to the kitchen and returned with a plate of *rava kesari*, his favourite sweet. Gopal was rather shocked. "Did you know about my promotion ?" He asked. "This sweet is not for your promotion." His mother said. "I too have got some good news for you and thought it best that I could inform you about the same with some sweet." While Gopal waited in eagerness, she began, "Today morning, after you left for office, Ramani's father had come to our house. He told me that he was willing to conduct the marriage very early along with fifty sovereigns of jewels." Gopal was even more excited with this news and thanked god that his wish was at last fulfilled.

Ramani proved to be the right choice. She was a good wife to Gopal and more so, a good daughter-in-law to his mother. Ramani's parents had advised her that she should consider her husband's mother as her own mother, and once she did this, she would never have a problem with her. Ramani had been very careful to follow their advice to the word and her mother-in-law was also very kind to her. At the beginning, she was scarred to leave her parents and enter a new home. But as time passed by, she realized that Gopal was kind-hearted and so was his mother and she never felt any difference between her home and her MIL's house.

Her honeymoon trip to Kodaikanal was a memorable one to her. They spent a week there and Ramani wondered, if all men loved their wives in this manner. She even wondered how, people ever thought of divorcing each other, after spending the time so closely together. Every evening, Gopal took her to temples, or a film. She thought of herself as the most lucky woman on earth. Life was a bed of roses to her.

But one had to face the thorns of life too. And for Ramani, the time had come to confront with it right away. Early one morning, when Ramani was chatting with Gopal, in the portico, her MIL barged in. She handed over a letter to her son and said, "Your sister is coming here next month for the vacation, along with her kids. Now, the time has come for you to fulfill the promise you had made to me, a few years ago."

Kamala had shelled out a major chunk of her savings towards purchase of the land in Chennai City. And with the remaining money she had, she was able to construct only a single bed room house. When her son settled in a job, she started pestering him to construct an extra room. But Gopal kept evading her request, telling her that, the house was roomy for three people and there was no necessity for an additional room. When his sister got married, Kamala insisted that the couple needed some privacy and brought up the matter once again. Gopal resolved the issue by sleeping in the hall. And even after that, whenever his sister came to meet them, he would clear out the bed room for them. But now, he was married and he could not tell his wife to sleep in the hall. He repented that he should have listened to his mother.

When Kamala told him that he had to construct an additional room immediately, he agreed. He convinced her that he would apply for a loan and within a month begin the construction work. But his mother retorted sharply, "Your sister is coming here next month, which means hardly twenty days are left. If you wait for the loan, you will begin construction only at the time of her departure. I request you to arrange money within two days and begin construction this Sunday itself, which is an auspicious day too."

"Constructing an additional room, as you think, is not that easy, mother. With the high inflation around, I need at least one lakh rupees to construct the room and where do I go for such a huge sum? I don't have any Godfather to pay me such a vast sum within another two days", he shouted.

But she was adamant. "Well, I have an idea. You just apply for the loan right away and let it take its own time for the amount to reach us. In the meanwhile, you can ask your wife to part with her jewels and pledge the same. Once you get the loan amount, you can redeem the jewels and give it to her."

All the while, Ramani had been sitting silently without interfering in their conversation. When at last, she heard her mother-in-law's suggestion, her blood began to boil. She began to think, it was for this, that she had demanded such a huge dowry. She remembered how her parents had led a very economical life, and even at the time of acute financial crisis, never did her father mortgage the jewels. How dare she asks her to part with the jewels, that to, hardly six months after her wedding. What rights had she on these jewels. How selfish woman was she, who was asking her to part with the jewels for the sake of her daughter.

As the waves of hatred left her, a sudden fear engulfed her. She realized that, if she refused to give her jewels now, a misunderstanding would arise between her and her MIL and this would continue for life long. She did not want to lead a life, where she was being cursed day in and day out, by her MIL. This may slowly result in her MIL spoiling her son's mind too and her marital life would become a failure. Her thoughts were disturbed when her mother-in-law asked her, "can you bring the jewels my dear, I shall take the entire responsibility of redeeming them within two months ?" Running inside, even without looking at her husband nor seeking his opinion, Ramani collected all her jewels and handed it over to her MIL and she in turn passed it on to her son.

Next day, after seeing her husband off to work, Ramani had entered the bedroom and shut the door behind her. She lay down on the bed and started crying. She realized that God had made her too happy for the past six months, only to bring about its doom very soon. The time had come for her marriage to be shattered. Her imagination turned wild and she dreaded what the evening was going to be like. What would her husband do, once he found out that out of the fifty sovereigns that she had given him, ten sovereigns were fake jewels. He would come home in the evening and was going to bash at her first. He would then berate her and call her father a cheat. And not only this, he would definitely express his wish to divorce her too. Ramani lay sobbing in self-pity. She was helpless now and she could do nothing. She never expected that the cat would be let cut of the bag so soon. She could have stopped such a catastrophe, befalling her but she had been selfish to see her wedding through. Had she been bold enough and stopped her father that day, things would have been different. Now, she had to pay for her silence, for indirectly, she had also been a part of the whole game.

It was one Thursday afternoon, when she returned from the library. She lifted her hand to press the calling bell, but stopped, on noticing that the door was half opened. She was about to step inside the house, when she heard her father's voice. She wondered why father had come home so early. Her parents were having a serious discussion and she heard her name being mentioned quite often. Ramani stepped aside and strained her ears to listen to what they were talking. Her father was telling her mother, "Chidambaram Gold Covering in Mambalam is a famous shop and today evening I shall buy the jewels from there. Remember, don't tell a word of this to anybody ." Ramani understood that her father was going to buy fake jewels to conduct the marriage. She wanted to tell them to cancel the marriage but she remained silent and stood there still, not knowing what exactly she had to do. Just then, she heard her father continue, "Don't tell this even to Ramani ; she might get upset. With my retirement money, I shall replace all the fake jewels." She then gave out a long sigh of relief. So, father was going to replace the fake jewels after all. She had often heard elders say, "There is nothing wrong in telling a thousand lies, to see the fruition of a marriage". She rationalized that, in her case, her father was just telling a single lie, and that was not a sin at all.

Also, she realized that if she interfered and stopped the marriage, by telling her father that she did not wish to marry a man, who attached more importance to dowry, she would be hurting him as well as her mother. Her father would feel ashamed that his daughter was aware of his swindling and he would repent for this act all his life. Her mother who was a heart patient, would get another massive attack. She remembered the quarrels they had everyday over her marriage. She would yell at the laxity of her father, "My daughter has already turned Twenty Five and still you have not been able to find a husband for her. I think it is not in my destiny to see my daughter's wedding." But her father would never get provoked. He would then humbly say, "Marriages are settled by God and unless the right time arrives, all our efforts only turn out to be futile." Now that the time had arrived for her marriage to take place, she did not wish to be a barrier to this by complicating the issue further and decided, not to get involved in any manner and left everything to her parents. It is they who are answerable to whatever happens to her in the future, and so she was determined to remain reticent on this.

After crying for so long, the tears had cooled her agitated mind and the feverish feeling had also gone. All of a sudden, a passion of courage swept across her. She realized that there was no point in crying like a chicken. She got emboldened and decided to act. She was of course aware that when Gopal returned, he was going to be enraged. She did not want to argue with him or give any justification. Being the only daughter, she wanted to protect her parents and did not wish to give them away. The worst that could happen, was a separation and so with this in mind, she began gathering all her belongings and started stuffing them into her suitcase. If her husband was going to be rude to her, she would walk out of his life that very instant.

It was twilight already and the "Allah-oh-Akbar" prayer song, was blaring in the nearby mosque. It was time for Gopal's return and though Ramani had taken a firm decision, she was filled with a sudden fright at what might happen from a short while from now. Her heart began to pound, when she heard the squeal of the motorbike and she walked into the kitchen, and pretended to be busy.

Gopal entered the house with a big packet in his hand. He just handed over the packet to his mother and immediately came out looking for her and said, "Darling, could you please come with a cup of coffee, my head is pounding." Ramani rushed to him with the coffee cup. He gulped down the coffee along with a painkiller. He told her that he was not keeping well and fell asleep. Ramani silently continued preparing dinner and she learnt that her mother-in-law had got the money required for commencing the construction, as she was beaming around with happiness. Even while having dinner, Gopal was calm and never uttered anything about the fake jewels. That night, Ramani did not sleep. She could not believe the way things were progressing and one thing she was sure of, was that a miracle had taken place and God had saved her from a mishap.

The next day, Ramani told her mother-in-law that she wished to do some shopping and went to see her mother. She decided that the time had come now for extinguishing the fire of chaos running through her mind. Though she had a feeling that her marriage was settled in heaven and she had been lucky to get the best husband in the world, her mind was clouded with a fear which cropped up from time to time. Ever since, she had overheard the conversation regarding the fake jewels her parents had, she was in dilemma. One part of her mind was always advising her to talk it out with her parents and get things cleared and the other was admonishing her not to hurt them, by letting them know that she was aware of their act and make them feel guilty of the same. The next moment, her mind would be filled with wild fantasies about Gopal learning the truth of the fake jewels and harassing her, followed by her walking out of his life. Her MIL's requisition of her jewels was the last straw on the camel's back. Even now, after what had happened, if she remained silent, without getting things straightened out with her mother, she was a moron. And so, today, on her way to her mother's house, she decided to break the ice. On reaching her house, she found that the door was locked. She sat down on the veranda, petrified. Her worst fears began to race through her mind. *May be my parents are already aware of the latest developments at home. And now, fearing that I would be returning after a quarrel with my husband, the two of them had probably run away, ashamed to face their daughter.* The clanging noise almost startled her from her fantasy and she saw her mother, entering with a basket of vegetables.

Ramani was excited to see her mother and she dragged her inside. She informed her that she had come here, to sort out a problem, which was killing her day in and day out. She appraised the whole story, from the time of overhearing the conversation between her parents till the pledging of the jewels. After listening to Ramani, her mother felt sorry that her daughter had experienced a very tough time all the while and repented that, had she divulged everything to Ramani in the beginning itself, she would have been spared from so much of mental torture. She asked her daughter to relax a little, then began narrating to her the other side of the story. "My dear girl, I am afraid, you are so much worked up over nothing. It is indeed very unfortunate that you had heard only half the story and had been worrying yourself all these days. Having overhead the conversation, you should have been prudent enough, to at least have got your doubts clarified. The inhibition on your part has resulted in such a confusion and you have been unnecessarily tormenting yourself. How could you ever believe that your father would have daringly done such a thing? To tell you the truth, it was your husband who gave us such an idea. Before the marriage, when Gopal learnt that your father did not wish to proceed further with this alliance because he was short of ten sovereigns, as demanded by your MIL, immediately, he went to your father's office and pleaded him to change his mind about dropping this alliance, as he liked you very much, and he also told him that he did not care for the ten sovereigns at all. He further advised your father to buy fake jewels, just to please his mother. However, your father did not agree to this, and told him, that he would replace the fake jewels, soon after his retirement. Gopal was very particular that no one, not even you, should know about it and hence pleaded with your father to keep it a secret. But somehow, father could not hold this from me and by hearing just part of the story, you had put yourself into too much of turmoil."

Ramani could not believe this and she froze cold with shock. In the days, when men were filled with greed and wished to confiscate everything possible at the time of marriage, she marveled at the fact, that her husband was so great a gentleman. She was indeed the most luckiest woman, to get a husband like Gopal. The little enactment played by her husband to get the girl of his choice and at the same time to satisfy his mother, was indeed a sublime feat. She was filled with an immense love for him, and immediately took a vow, to be a loving wife and a pleasing daughter-in-law, all her life. A wonderful glow of happiness suffused her whole body, and as if to take part in the pleasure, her baby was kicking her inside the womb. Stroking her tummy, she said, you have a great father and one day, I will tell you the story of your father, and his love he had for your mother - the love story of a unique kind !

6

The Obliging Husband

It was almost 3 o'clock when Ashok returned to his room, after inspecting the machinery in his factory. Now he felt rather elated as he had found the probable reasons for the low production, in the last quarter, which had resulted in low sales. Pulling out his scrapbook, he began jotting down the points to prepare a report, enumerating the various causes, one after another. After getting set, he buzzed in for his secretary, to dictate the report. But all of a sudden, he heard a rumbling noise in his stomach, a sign that his body required some food. Today, he came early to the office, skipping his usual breakfast in order to complete this project and without even carrying his lunch along with him. At noon also, he had a quick bite of sandwiches and now he was really famished.

Curious to know what his wife was planning for dinner, he rang home. Preetha was rather surprised to hear her husband's voice, for he hardly calls her from office, except during emergencies. When he asked her about the menu for dinner, she at once decided to prepare his favourite dish and blurted, "It is chappatis and channa tonight." As he heard that, his mouth watered and he informed her that he would be home before seven o'clock.

Just as Preetha entered the kitchen to soak the channa, she heard the doorbell chime. When she opened the door, she saw her daughter there with a brooding face and slightly hunching due to the load of books in her bag. When Preetha asked her why she was in a very grumpy mood, Sona implored, "Ma, today, I have a lot of homework to do besides preparing for two tests. If you can please help me with the homework part, I shall then be free to study for my tests tomorrow." Seeing the pleading look, Preetha agreed to help her daughter. She sat down with her who explained in detail the different homework to be done. Requesting for a pen, she commenced her work. The difficult task was not doing her daughter's homework, but writing it out, in her style, which was very much time consuming. Sona happily prepared for her tests, while Preetha was slogging with the homework. After she was done with her job, she stretched out her hands and legs, when suddenly her eyes fell on the clock. The time was 6.45 p.m. She immediately got up with a jolt.

She ran into the kitchen and wondered whether she will be able to cook anything before the arrival of her husband. She cursed herself for her poor memory. Ashok had indeed been right about her getting old. Since he could be at home any moment now, Preetha panicked, for she knew that when her husband was hungry, he was angry too. Immediately after his return from the office, if dinner was delayed for some reason or the other, he would become irked and start nagging her. Preetha had learnt it the hard way, to serve him food at the appropriate time, come what may.

Trying to avoid a quarrel, she decided to make a simple dinner. She remembered that there was a little idli flour in the fridge. Eager to finish her work before her husband's return, she quickly poured the flour into the idli moulds and placed them in the cooker. This time when the doorbell rang, she called out her daughter to attend it and continued with her work. As Ashok entered, he was excited to have his favourite dinner. After getting fresh, he sat at the dining table and ordered his wife to bring his food. His temper roused when he saw a plate of idlis placed in front of him, and he shouted, "What made you change the menu all of a sudden ?"

"Your daughter took all my time. I was busy doing her homework and forgot all about the dinner," she said apologetically.

"Well, as usual your daughter comes first. I have got no place of importance here," he grumbled.

Preetha was not willing to listen to his grouches, so she cut him short by saying, "If you can give me some time, I shall prepare your favourite dish, in a jiffy."

Ashok, who was stubborn and willing to have his way, immediately stood up and left the dining table without having the idlis and insisted that she call him only after making the chappatis.

For the next hour, Preetha remained busy in preparing the dinner and it was 8.30 p.m., when she requested her husband to have his dinner. Ashok, who had been starving the whole day, now devoured up the chappatis, one after another, appreciating his wife's cooking all the while.

After his hunger was appeased, he felt sorry for rebuking her. To apologise, he entered the kitchen, stood by her side and gently said, "If such delicious preparations were available in any of the hotels around here, I would have not bothered you at all. Who can cook so delectably, but my wife." Preetha shoved off his hands from her shoulder and said, "Don't try to cool me, understand. I know how heartless and uncaring you could be at times. I am in no mood to listen to your sweet words and now please leave me alone for some time."

But Ashok was not going to leave her. If he did not try to calm her, she would get into a surly mood and this would get into his nerves.

"Darling, I am sorry, if I had been harsh to you. Tell me what I should do to please you? I will definitely carry it out to the word." He breathed into her ears.

Preetha, who was still boiling inside, retorted, "If that is the case, then I want you to go and hang yourself."

Without uttering another word, Ashok left the room. Preetha continued her work peacefully.

After having her dinner, Preetha began scrubbing the oily pans and plates. Her daughter was sitting in the hall, still studying for her tests and Preetha decided to help her out with a few tips, after completing her work. In the end, she looked around for the rag cloth, to clean the kitchen counter, which was her last ritual for the day. As she forcibly moved the rag cloth to and fro, across the counter, her thoughts shifted to her husband.

Suddenly her hands began to tremble and the worst fears came into her mind. What if her husband had taken her bickering a little too seriously and had carried out her command. The fact that the place was so silent, and she had not seen him around for the past half an hour, made her heart to throb. Automatically some previous incidents, came into her mind.

There had been a gap of four months between her engagement and wedding and so, on Saturday afternoons, Ashok would take her out to either the park or the beach, just to while away their time. On the Saturday, just before their wedding, Preetha had been waiting for almost one hour at the bus stop and still there was no sign of Ashok. She got very impatient and she started to walk along the pavement slowly. Just then, she heard somebody was frantically honking behind her. When she turned back she saw her would-be husband. But Preetha continued to walk without paying any particular attention to him, as if he was somebody on the road. Immediately, Ashok knew that she was angry with him due to his delay. He drove ahead of her and parked his vehicle in front of her in order to block her way. Preetha stood there with a sullen face, without looking at him. Ashok gave her a proper justification for his delay and apologized to her very humbly. It was only then that her face lit up a little. However, her normal cheerfulness was missing, for still she remained grumpy. But Ashok was determined to bring that smile back on her face, so he said, "Once again,

I reiterate that I am sorry for the undue delay, madam. Now tell me, what I ought to do, to see your bright face." Preetha wished to have some fun. A bus was standing near them which was ready to move. After the conductor blew his whistle, signaling the driver to start moving, she said, "Well, stop that bus for me right now, so that I could board it and reach home."

Immediately, Ashok put his two fingers into his mouth and whistled aloud and all of a sudden, the bus which had advanced a short distance, came to an abrupt halt. The conductor, a rude man, annoyed at this interruption, came out, enquiring, as to who had stopped the bus. Preetha was rather perplexed at what was happening around her. As the conductor came toward them, she saved her would-be husband by saying, "Well, it was for me that he stopped the bus."

"Then why are you standing here, get into the bus ?" he yelled.

Preetha after mumbling something into Ashok's ears immediately ran into the bus. She got down at the third stopping, where Ashok had been waiting and as he saw her, he gave out a loud laugh and Preetha too could not control her laughter.

From then, it had always been like that. Though Ashok was a short-tempered man and blasted at his wife for the slightest vexation, he was also a soft-natured and obliging husband. For very soon, he would repent for his strident behaviour and try his best to compromise with her. Often, Preetha would get morose and avoid him, as much as possible. But Ashok never liked to see her in that gloomy mood. Many a times, he would go all out to placate her and wipe out that sullenness from her face, by readily obliging to all her whims and fancies. Using this compromise technique of her husband, Preetha had obtained many favours from him. On several occasions, she had demanded things like, costly necklace, beautiful saree, golden watch, or sometimes, an outing to the theatre or the hotel to skip the usual cooking at home.

Throwing the scrub into the sink, she made haste to the bedroom. With a pounding heart, she forcibly opened the door of the bedroom and found her husband reclined on the bed with his favourite news magazine. She gave out a long sigh of relief. On seeing the petrified look on her face, Ashok at once knew the cause. Straightening up from bed, he leapt out and grabbed her hand and asked, "Were you petrified that I was out, complying with your order ? As long as it helps to see that beautiful smile on your face, I would indeed do anything on earth, however flimsy it might be ; but when it results in our separation, I am not a damned fool to oblige you. After all, I love you so dearly and cannot afford to miss you anytime." Preetha stood their listening to his pacifying words, and seeing the blush on her face, he drew her close to himself.

7

The Prediction

Rupa was eagerly waiting for her husband. It was her first wedding anniversary, and she felt rather upset that her husband had not even purchased a saree to mark the occasion, leave alone, a gala celebration. However, she did not wish to dispute with him over his slackness. She deliberated that, had he not intervened in her life, she would have been an insane person by now. So, when Krishnan stepped out of the house, for his college, she meekly reminded him, that it was their first wedding anniversary. He replied to her in the same tone, that he remembered too and left for his college, without uttering another word. Krishnan was a man of few words, and even after spending a year closely with this man, Rupa could not comprehend as to what type of man was her husband. However, she held him in high esteem and to her he was the Almighty who had saved her life from wreck.

While driving to his college that day, Krishnan thought about his friends, who made a big show on their wedding anniversaries by spending lavishly. They tried to exhibit their love and admiration for their wives in all possible manner. And he reasoned that there was no need for him to flaunt to his wife, as he loved her dearly, every day of the year. For he had never been rude to her even once, from his very first association with her, five years ago and Rupa too continued to be like the meek and obedient student of his, ever since. As he drove ahead, he began reminiscing the past....

The very first time he saw her, he suspected that she was some kind of a lunatic and felt sorry that such a beautiful and young girl was insane. He even wondered as to why God was so merciless at times. After giving tuitions to the boys, he was just proceeding outwards, when all of a sudden, he caught a glimpse of a young girl in total rags, with disheveled hair, digging the earth with a stick. As he started his bike, the girl looked up and smiled at him. The next day, he got a closer view of the girl. She was standing near the barbed wire fence, staring at him, eager to start a conversation with him. He also noticed that she was dressed better than the previous day and her hair was done up neatly. On the third day, as he started to leave, the girl waved to him, beckoning him. But Krishnan drove off quietly.

A few days later, he was rather flabbergasted when he saw her standing close to his bike, nicely attired. As he was about to start his bike, she ran up to him and squatting on the ground, held his feet tightly. Krishnan, who had till now remained mute to all her gestures, wished to respond politely.

"Tell me what is it that you want from me ?", he asked in a soft tone.

Amidst sobs, the girl said, "If only you promise·to fulfil my wish, I shall let off your feet."

Not getting an immediate answer, Rupa continued to linger on. It was his innocent and kind looks that had steered her and also emboldened her to take such a drastic step. In fact, she was guided by her inner conscious which kept admonishing her that this was exactly the person sent by God, in answer to her prayers, who could help her out of the darkness.

Her pleading looks melted Krishnan's heart and he realized that the girl was a victim of Fate's wild blows and promised to help her out, if only, it was within his capability and limits.

Then, Rupa narrated to him, the whole story, which was boiling inside her for almost a year and Krishnan was all ears to her grievances. After giving a patient hearing, he said, "well, I shall come to your house tomorrow and talk to your mother and see if I can change her mind."

Rupa was thrilled to hear these words and thanked him profusely.

Rupa was the most brilliant student in her class. She stood first in the school in her Plus Two Board Examination. After completion of school, she wished to graduate in Botony due to her love for nature and hence applied to different colleges. She received a positive reply from all the colleges and was now in a fix as to which one to join.

It was during this time that one of her far relative's son came to see her and was pleased with her beautiful looks. The boy's mother started pressing for an early marriage and Rupa's mother requested for a few months' time to arrange for the wedding. Meanwhile, Rupa protested that she wished to complete her graduation first and then find a job, before contemplating on marriage. But her mother convinced her that she had personally spoken to the boy and he had promised that he would let her to continue her studies even after marriage. And so, Rupa reluctantly agreed for the marriage, without further arguments.

One early morning, Rupa's mother set off to her home town with the horoscopes of her daughter and the bridegroom to meet her family astrologer, who was now an Octogenarian. Before commencement of all auspicious occasions in the family, he was consulted for his expert opinion and based on his suggestions only, she would take her next step. After comparing the two horoscopes, the old man became sullen. Then, he said pathetically, "Both these horoscopes don't match well." Her heart broke and her desire of getting her daughter married off very soon was shattered.

Then, she asked the next question which was in her mind, "As per her horoscope, when is the appropriate time for the marriage ?"

The old man did not answer her. Thinking that he had not heard her, she repeated the question once again.

"To tell you the truth, you will never see your daughter's wedding," he said.

On seeing the petrified look on her face, he clarified it to her, "I mean, there won't be any necessity for you to conduct your daughter's marriage, for according to this horoscope, your daughter would elope with a man of her choice."

The old man's prediction was more of a shock to her and she sat there transfixed not knowing what to do.

On her way back, she kept brooding over the next step she had to take with regard to her daughter. Then slowly, an idea came to her mind. She was happy that at last she knew how to tackle the problem on hand. She knew that one should be bold enough to flee with a man, abandoning the family ties. This courage emnates only when one becomes independent in life. She reasoned that her daughter can become self-supporting only if she finished her graduation and went for a job. Hence, she decided then and there, to stop educating her further and train her in house work and cooking. In the mean time, she would hastily set about finding a suitable boy for her and settle the wedding and wash off her hands. At last, she felt relieved at her resolution and reached home happily.

Rupa was bubbling with excitement the whole day. Her neighbour's daughter Kalpana was the student of Meenakshi College and she was doing her final year in Botony there. She advised Rupa to join the same, because of its good reputation and qualified teaching staff. And Rupa was waiting to inform this to her mother with great eagerness.

But when, she found her mother in a very disturbed mood she decided to open the topic a little later. Rupa was much perturbed on finding her mother so depressed and wondered what the reason could be. In the evening, her mother called her and conveyed to her about the drastic decision that she had taken. She lied to her that since the horoscopes matched very well, she had gone to meet the boy's mother and communicated the happy news. While discussing with her, she learnt that the old woman expected a huge dowry which she could not afford and so cancelled the alliance right away. And that is why she is now forced to stop her education to save a considerable amount for her marriage. She further advised her that she could postpone her studies until after marriage and drop it for now.

Rupa knew her mother too well. Once she had taken a decision, there was no way that you could change her mind. Knowing of her stubbornness, Rupa did not say a word to her mother. As usual, she abided by her decision and silently collected all the papers and tore them into shreds and threw them into the bin. As she did this, a wild hatred grew towards her mother. Her mother's decision was inhuman and she regretted that there was not a single soul on this earth who could question her savage decision.

Within a few months, a total metamorphosis took over Rupa. She never gave thought of what she ate or wore. Nor did she bother to keep herself clean, her hair was tangled and unkempt always. Her intake reduced considerably too and she became pale and thin. Day in and day out she yearned to go to college and study, like the other girls in the neighbourhood. She had been dreaming of going for a job after graduation and helping her mother, who had been running the family single-handedly with her father's pension. But all her dreams had gone up in smoke.

In the mornings, when the streets were busy with school children and college girls, she would start envying them. Immediately she would get inside and close all the windows and start banging the walls with her fists, until they ached, for being deprived of such a life. Day by day, her health and beauty were deteriorating. She looked very haggard and weak. The boys who came to see her did not like her and her marriage got invariably delayed for one reason or the other.

Though her mother was aware of the change in her, she remained tacit and pretended to be oblivious to the fact and did not wish to raise the matter. She only hoped that Rupa would gradually get used to the changed life style. But when all the young men who came to see her, expressed their unwillingness to wed her, due to her worn-out condition, she became concerned over her daughter's future, for whom, she had been alive so long.

Rupa's condition worried her a lot and she decided to take her to the temple everyday, to invoke the Goddess's blessing for an early marriage. On one such occasion, she chanced to meet her neighbour Kalpana, who was really shocked to see her.

"Are you not keeping well ?", she asked.

Rupa timidly shook her head. Suddenly, her eyes welled up. Here was some one who really cared for her and immediately words flowed out from her mouth. She confessed everything to her. After listening to her, Kalpana's heart ached. She exploded, "Had you told me about this, I would have helped you earlier. But still we have time. If your mother does not like to borrow from anyone, there is another option. A new master is coming to my house these days to teach my brothers. He is kind-hearted and after his tuitions, my unruly brothers have changed and their marks have also gone higher. I heard from my father that he is a do-gooder and has helped many a student in his college by giving financial help. He is known for his benevolence and charity and if you request him, he would definitely help you too, for you have scored first in your school and the master likes brilliant students."

Rupa listened to her friend's advice, with a throbbing heart. At last, time has come for a change in her life and she started planning her next course of action.

The next day, Rupa kept prancing across the room, staring at the clock excitedly. When the hands of the clock turned to 6 p.m., she came into the garden and stood their waiting for an opportunity to meet the master. But once she saw him emerge out, her throat became dry and she did not know how to begin her conversation with him. Somehow, she felt relieved that she did not talk to him, for she noticed that she was wearing a tattered *churidhar* and was not dressed properly.

The next day, she was very cautious and wore her favourite *churidar* and came up to the barbed wire fence and stood there, wishing to talk to him. As he came out, she gathered up all her courage, but he had left without heeding to her. A few days later, one fine evening, she prayed God for his blessings and looking her best, she came out of the fence and stood there near his bike. On seeing him, she was scared stiff and not knowing what to say, she squatted on the floor and held his feet. For she did not know any other way to impress him best in achieving her goal. And the master had patiently listened to her woes and promised to meet her mother and have a talk with her and see to it that she continued her study.

The following day, Rupa was washing the vessels at the backyard, when she heard the door bell. She was sure that it would be none other than the master and her heart started beating faster. However, she continued with her work and never dared to enter the hall. The young man introduced himself to Rupa's mother, as Krishnan, the college professor and the tutor of the boys in the neighbourhood and comfortably sat down on the sofa. He then told her in brief about the purpose of his visit, "Learning that your daughter despite obtaining the first position in school, is unable to continue her studies due to the pecuniary condition, I have come to help her out. Our college grants scholarships to the bright students and I shall talk to the principal and arrange for a scholarship for your daughter."

Though Rupa's mother was delighted to hear that the master was willing to help her daughter, she alone knew that money was not the real problem. She, somehow, felt that revealing the truth to this man would do more good than harm and she would also be absolved from the blame of selfishness. Gingerly, she let the cat out of the bag. She narrated the truth to the teacher. She also admitted that actually she had been self-centered of losing her daughter, apart from the fear that she would be castigated by the neighbours and her own relatives for not raising her daughter in the proper manner.

After hearing her story, Krishnan was rather amazed that in the cyber age, there still lived such gullible people. He then stated a story which had converted him into a non-believer in astrology. "I was once compelled by my friend to accompany him to an astrologer. He took his horoscope along with him and wished to know from him, as to how his future would be. But after what I saw there, I silently left the place and also lost faith in the so-called predictions. The astrologer had three children. The first two were girls and the third was a boy. Unfortunately, the boy was born with Down's syndrome and he kept hobbling around his father, who in turn was hollering at him to go to his room. I began to wonder, that if he was a reputed and good astrologer as presumed by everyone in the neighbourhood, he must have known about the future of his own child and should have avoided the birth. This clearly shows that there is no one above the Almighty who alone controls and shapes our lives. Nothing can happen to us until He wishes, and anyone having full faith in Him, need not fear anything about the predictions of the so-called astrologers, who are after all ordinary human beings like you and me. It was then that I decided never to believe in astrology or any kind of foretelling." Before leaving, he said, "It is you, who have brought up your daughter with great love and understanding and how can you ever fail to trust your own daughter ?" Rupa's mother was silent and did not have an answer for this.

The words of the master kept ringing in her ears. She now recalled her early life. It was the same astrologer, to whom her father had consulted at the time of her marriage. After comparing the two horoscopes, he had forecasted that they matched very well and that the couple would lead a happy marital life for a long period. The words of the astrologer had proved to be a total fallacy. Unfortunately, her husband met with an accident and she was destined to live with him only for hundred days. Since then, she had been single-handedly fending for herself and her daughter. Thus, Rupa had not even seen her father and she was brought up solely by her.

The Master had now opened her mind to the realities. She felt sorry that she had ill-treated her loving daughter, heeding to the predictions of the astrologer, who had once given a false conclusion about her life. She decided that her daughter's life should not be ruined further and made all the arrangements for her further studies.

The hatred that Rupa was harbouring towards her mother was ironed out, for she had realised that her mother had after all been too possessive of her. Fearing separation from her loving daughter and the bad name it would bring to her, she had acted like that. She was so grateful to the master for his interference and sorting out the problem, thereby changing her whole life. Rupa continued to study in good earnest, worthy of the scholarship that was awarded to her and it was during her final year in college, that she was taken in for a wide surprise.

One evening, Rupa was preparing coffee, when all of a sudden she saw Kalpana's mother enter the door. She was rather shocked, because the old lady never left the house, except on important occasions. On seeing her, Rupa began to wonder, what could be the reason for her visit. Her mother greeted the old woman and asked her to sit down on the sofa. After comfortably sitting in the sofa, she spoke at length about Kalpana's wedding and regretted that Rupa had not attended the marriage. Slowly, she opened the topic of Rupa's marriage, "Are you not serious about getting your daughter married soon ?"

Rupa's mother gave out a long sigh. "There is no suitable boy from my side." She said. "The three of them, whom I had been contemplating all the while, have seen Rupa already and refused to marry her, a few years back. Out of them, one of the boy is still unmarried, but Rupa is not interested in him, as he had refused her once."

Kalpana's mother immediately broke the news, for which purpose she had come down all the way, "Yesterday, the master came to our house. He informed us about his transfer to his home town, Pondicherry. When I asked him about his family, he said that both his parents were gone and he had no siblings too. When I further coaxed him about marriage, he said that he was planning to advertise in the newspaper shortly. I gather that he belongs to the same caste as yours, and if you are willing, we can talk it out and settle Rupa's marriage with him."

Generally, Rupa's mother would have told that the horoscopes should match first, before proceeding with the marriage, but now, she had lost the entire faith in astrology and foretellings and immediately exclaimed, "If only that young man agrees to marry Rupa, I am confident that my daughter would be the luckiest girl on this earth."

And within six months, Rupa tearfully bid farewell to her mother, to Pondicherry, along with her husband, who had first reformed her and then wedded her.

Krishnan was in the middle of his lecture, when the peon entered and informed him of the phone call. Anxious to know, as to who was trying to contact him during this time of the day, he scurried across to the staff room, and picked up the phone. When he spoke into the phone, his face lit with a smile, as he heard the familiar voice of Kalpana's brothers who were vying with each other to wish him on his first wedding anniversary. Setting the receiver on the craddle, he started marvelling at the fact that, these days, even the youngsters knew that the wedding day was a special day in the life of a married couple and appreciated the boys who had taken much pains to track him down somehow. He decided that he too had to please his wife on this very special day and immediately on reaching home, he asked Rupa if she had any plans of celebrating the wedding day.

"Not really !" Said Rupa excitedly. "To me, spending each day with you is itself a matter of great celebration and joy. And my only wish is to enjoy this bliss and your love for ever."

Krishnan's face lit up with a smile on hearing the words and he assured her of his everlasting love towards her.

8

The Cage Bird

Raju was looking outside the window, gazing at the setting sun. Today he came early from work. Only now did he realize that it was all his fault and had he controlled his temper on that night and not hit his wife, he would have been a happy man. It had been a month since his wife and son had left him. Since then, he had not bothered, even to phone up to Prema or meet his son. Somehow, he felt that his ego and temperament have smashed his life.

His was an arranged marriage. He was born and brought up in a village. He studied engineering and then shifted to the Chennai city, where he had been offered a job. He got married with Prema. After marriage Raju took his wife to Ooty for the honeymoon. Prema was captivated by the natural beauty in Ooty. She expressed her happiness to her husband, who promised many more such pleasure trips in the future. But very soon, she learnt that it was a false promise for she found out that her husband was a workaholic.

Prema had always wished to enjoy the outside world ; the freedom of which was denied to her in her village, where sending girls to school was a taboo. However, it was her elder brother, who insisted that she had to go to school and further sent her to college. Although every time, she was accompanied by her father or brother. On some days, Prema would be tempted to dress up in a fashionable manner and go to the college. But then her mother would comment, "Modest girls" don't attire themselves brightly, attracting every one. You may do so, after getting married. Why let people wag their tongues, unnecessarily now ?"

Prema would think of retorting, that those days have gone. Nowadays, women are out in every field, even flying aeroplanes ; but finally would decide not to. After all, her mother had told her that she was free to adorn herself after marriage. Secretly, she kept praying, for her marriage to take place. She had been dreaming to visit various places, embellished in different style everyday, to please her husband and make him feel proud of her.

Being a Construction Engineer, Raju's job kept him away from home. His company was undertaking major construction works in the city and he would spend most of the time either supervising a concreting job or monitoring the fabrication work. Everyday, Raju would leave early in the morning and return late in the night. Prema would be lounging all alone in the bungalow, waiting for his arrival. One day, she requested him to take her out for a movie and he promised to come home early with the tickets. Prema stood in front of the wardrobe for a very long time deciding what to wear. Finally, she selected her favourite dress and spent a lot of time in front of the mirror doing her make-up and hair do. Raju had promised to pick her up at six o'clock. When the hands of the clock turned six, she became restless, and kept peeping outside, to see if he had arrived. *Raju is going to be stunned, on seeing me*, she thought.

Prema waited in vain up to 10 p.m. When he returned, he found that his wife was in a grumpy mood. Immediately, he apologized to her, "Just when I was about to leave, my boss called me up and handed me a special assignment. When I tried to explain to him that I had to go home early, he told me that the matter was urgent and he wished to discuss with me right away. I had no other go." He then promised to take her for the movie on Sunday. Prema did not wish to quarrel with him and quickly compromised. However, they were not able to go out that weekend too, for Raju was called up by his boss once again.

Prema was annoyed that her husband was returning late almost everyday. It was getting on her nerves and she decided to do something about it immediately. She had to act and if she remained a silent spectator to whatever he was doing, she would have to be a cage bird all her life. That day, when Raju returned home, he found Prema was in a sulky mood and did not get out of bed to even serve him dinner. Raju, thinking that his wife was unwell, helped himself with the dinner and later relaxed in front of the television. Slowly, Prema got out of the bed and walked up to him.

Sitting beside him, she asked, "Don't you love me?"

Shocked to hear that, Raju asked, "what makes you think so?"

"Because, you are always away from home. You don't bother to spend time with me. Somehow, I get a feeling that my marriage was settled in hell and not in heaven. For all my dreams of roaming around freely with my husband has got shattered. If work is all that matters, why did you ever think of marriage?"

"Tell me what exactly I should do ?" he yelled.

"Well, I want you at home by sharp 6 p.m., everyday. You have to sit with me and chat and also take me out to different places. You have to remove the lonely feeling I have been experiencing of late," she complained.

"Why don't you make friends with the neighbourhood ladies and while away your time with them ?"

"I don't need their friendship. I am starving of my husband's love and I need you sharp at 6 p.m., from tomorrow, come what may."

The next day, in the office, when the time was five o'clock, Raju was pondering over a problematic file, and all of a sudden, his wife's order came to his mind. Immediately, he closed his file and left the office. That day, on seeing her husband so early, Prema was thrilled and the entire evening was filled with fun. She was happy that at last, by sitting with her husband and talking out her mind, she was able to change him to her taste. However, she was vexed by the fact that he started bringing files with him and worked at home, till late night. But since the boredom of staying alone at home was gone, she did not comment on his working at home. But this satisfaction too, was only short-lived, for very soon, she had to encounter another problem of a different kind.

Raju had been requesting his boss for an additional hand, to assist him with the field trips. His boss had approved of it. After Pradeep joined him, Raju found that his task was halved. He would send Pradeep out for supervision jobs and swiftly clear up the paper work. Pradeep would return in the evening and apprise him about the progress of the projects at the various sites that he had inspected. One day, Pradeep returned late and Raju hence took him to his house. Pradeep briefed him about the latest developments. After that, Pradeep made it a point to frequently visit him at his residence. On some days, he even came home earlier and waited for him. In the beginning, Prema was not disturbed by it. Slowly, she got irked by his presence, for he lingered around till eight o'clock. Once again, she got enraged with her husband as he did not try to stop him. Somehow, she thought it wise not to complain to him about it. At least, he returned home early these days, when his presence was most required, for she was in the last leg of pregnancy.

It was their first wedding anniversary. Prema reminded him about the grand treat that he had promised to celebrate the special day. She told him that she would he ready in the evening and first they would be going to the temple followed by dinner in the five star hotel. Prema then rummaged the bureau and broke her head, as to how best to attire herself for the evening. Slowly, she picked out one saree after another and examined it after placing it over her body, and finally decided to wear the Maroon silk saree with large gold embroidery, the saree she wore on her wedding day. It took her two hours to get set and finally when she viewed herself in the mirror, she marveled that even on the wedding day, she did not look so gorgeous. She smiled to herself that, if Raju saw her with the heavy make-up, he was going to swoon at her beauty. But when he returned, her spirit fell ; for behind him, followed Pradeep with a huge file, full of enthusiasm to please his boss, and she tried hard to control all her emotions. On seeing her, Pradeep immediately apologized, "I shall not take much time, madam. This is an important tender document and I have got some doubts, which I would like to get cleared from boss, quickly."

Though they had discussed for almost an hour, they had not arrived at any concrete decision. It was a big project, for which they had to prepare the cost estimate and submit the tender. In the morning Raju had shown his draft proposal to his boss and he had commented that the rates quoted were on the higher side and advised him to reduce the rates further. So Raju had all the while been breaking his head as to how effectively could this be done. In achieving that goal, they had not been aware of the passing time and suddenly, when Raju looked up the clock, he was aghast, for the time was already eight o'clock. After seeing Pradeep off, he rushed in, to apologize to his wife for the delay.

The twilight had turned into deep darkness and Prema was getting impatient. She kept stomping in side her room angrily thinking that Raju would hear the sound of her anklets and be reminded of their outing, but he was so immersed in his discussion that he did not even turn around. As she was wearing a heavy make-up, she felt rather awkward to barge in front of the two men. At last, when it was eight o'clock, her temper was aroused and she decided that there was no point in getting the blessings of the Lord, at this hour of the day. At once, she doffed off her silk saree that she had been wearing and changed into a ragged nightie. Burying her head deep into the soft pillow, she was crying her grief away.

When Raju entered the room, he was dismayed at what he saw.

"Are we not going out for dinner ?" he asked

"I am not keeping well, and moreover, I don't think it is necessary to go out for dinner, when you have a nice cook at home !" she said, in between her sobs.

Raju understood that she was being sarcastic and he blurted, "Had you told me this a few minutes back, I could have at least finished my project satisfactorily."

Provoked by his careless rejoinder, she screamed, "I never thought that my life would be doomed in this manner. I had great expectations to lead a carefree life after marriage, but God had shattered all my dreams and I am destined to lead my life with a slipshod man, who is heartless." Raju paid no attention to her rumblings and left the room, without even trying to appease her. Of late, such unpleasant episodes were occurring too frequently and Prema decided that she had to do something about it and not let it continue. After considering it for a long while, she realized that Raju was a difficult person and she could never mould him, however much she tried. At last, she resolved to change her own attitude for a better and peaceful life. He had given her freedom to make friends with the neighbours and she decided to come out of her shell, to get rid of her loneliness and boredom.

Raju's slogging nature emanates from his upbringing. He had grown up in a joint family, where his grandfather was a landlord and his father assisted him in his daily activities. There was a constant influx of people all through the day and his grandfather and father were busy sorting out problems of one kind or the other. It could be some important advice to the workmen, regarding the time of reaping or sowing in the field or settling domestic quarrels between brothers regarding ancestral property or any other petty quarrels in the neighbourhood. Raju had seen his mother sweating out in the kitchen the whole day, without complaining. He remembered, how on some occasions, when the country bigwigs came to meet his father, he would call out to her, to bring in some coffee and snacks, and even before he finished uttering her name, his mother would be standing in front of him, eager to carry out his errands. To his mother, her husband and the family was the whole world and he had never seen her move out of the house. Having grown up in such an atmosphere, Raju could not comprehend Prema's craving to move around freely.

After having new friends in the neighbourhood, slowly Prema began enjoying her new freedom. She would herself go out to buy the vegetables from the market everyday and stopped sending the servant maid. She spent most of her time with the women in the neighbourhood and also started going out with them to the movies or the park. Many a time Raju returned home and found the door locked. To solve the problem, he got a duplicate key made. But he did not complain about it, for he felt relieved that he was now free to fully concentrate on his work, without disturbance.

But when Vikram was born, things changed altogether. Throughout the day, Prema spent her time tending her son and as he grew, she enjoyed his pranks and never had time for herself. The word "boring" was completely erased from her dictionary. Raju too enjoyed playing with his son. As soon as he returned home, Vikram would run to him and cry that he should be lifted. He would then demand him, "What did you buy for me today ?" Raju would then give him a chocolate and the little boy would be munching it for a long time. When dad was at home, Vikram would be too elated and keep tottering behind him. And when he left for work, he would run up to him and say, "Come soon in the evening and play with me." But Raju's nature had not altered at all. In fact, now, his job entailed him to go out on frequent tours too.

It was Vikram's third birthday, Prema had been planning to celebrate it in a grand manner, inviting all her relatives. Raju had also agreed to her suggestion, but a week before that, he was summoned by his boss and asked to go to Mumbai, for an important public tender opening, where his presence was much essential. Raju, too could not refuse it for it was he, who had prepared the documents and quotation for this tender. If this job was allotted to them, it could turn over the company's future. It was a job, involving crores of money and his boss had promised him a high rise in his pay, if this tender was awarded in their favour. Raju was very anxious of the result and he agreed to go for the tender opening. When he told this to Prema, she was very upset and dropped the idea of the birthday celebration. However, he promised that he would be returning late in the evening, on Vikram's birthday.

Vikram wore his new dress on his birthday and flaunted around in the neighbourhood, along with his mother, distributing chocolates. His daddy had promised him Cadbury chocolates on his birthday, and so once back home, he was reminded of his daddy and he started his usual tantrums for one thing or the other. Generally, Prema tried to be patient to all his outbursts but occasionally, when his screams would make her mad, she would silence him by whacking. But on his birthday, she wished to be kind to him and so pacified him by telling, "If you are a nice boy today, I shall take you out to the beach in the evening."

Immediately he stopped crying and his face brightened. "Are you sure, you won't cheat me like papa does ?" he asked enthusiastically.

"Only if you behave well and don't trouble mummy."

This trick worked out well as Vikram calmed down and started playing in his tricycle. Somehow, the whole day, there was tranquility around and Prema carried on her chore without much difficulty. As a birthday treat, she made *Mysore pak*, a sweet which Vikram adored much.

In the evening, Vikram became restive and kept pestering his mother to lock up the house and take him to the beach. It was almost six o'clock, when they stepped out of the house. Once on the road, she was looking for an auto, when all of a sudden, a car swept across her and halted in front of her house.

Prema stood there for a while to see who it was, and was rather shocked to see her husband's boss alighting from the car. He informed her, "Actually, just an hour ago, Raju telephoned me that he would be back at 6 p.m., and since I am leaving for my home town tonight, I thought I could meet him and get the full details of the tender, which was awarded in our favour."

For a moment, Prema stood there speechless. She did not know the appropriate way of answering her husband's boss. If she told him to wait for her husband's arrival, her presence was also a must, which meant that she had to cancel her son's pleasure trip. And she was determined, not to displease him, for she alone knew the pains of deception. While she was contemplating on what reply to give, he was quick to ask, "Can I wait here for sometime ?"

She had to take a decision right away and so she blurted, "Could you please come after some time as I am taking my son to the beach right now ?"

She was aware that she had disappointed him by speaking so rudely, but she had no regrets whatsoever. After all, he was the boss to her husband and not to her. All that mattered now, was her son, whose happiness she did not want to disrupt in any manner. She wanted to keep up her promise. Happy that she was able to take firm decision without wavering, she proceeded to the nearby auto stand. Vikram had a jolly time at the beach. He returned home, with balloons, kites and other small toys, which his mother bought for him at the beach.

Raju was at home, when both of them returned. Vikram at once, ran and cuddled his father. He was happy to see his father after a long time. However, Prema was quick to notice that he was furious over something. But she preferred to avoid him and entered the kitchen. After about an hour, Raju came in and pulled up a chair. Prema silently served him dinner. Slowly, he broke the ice, "How dare you drive out my boss like that ? Don't you know the etiquettes of treating people ? It is my fate that I am married to a village brute, who is not aware of the etiquettes of handling people. Had I married a city bred girl, she would have been polite and asked my boss in."

Prema was in fact dying to see her husband, for this was the first time, that he had been away for almost a week. She had been all the day planning to talk to him about whatever happened during his absence. She also wanted to boast about Vikram, who behaved so well on account of her promise to take him out to the beach. But his sharp words provoked her and she could feel the palpitation of her heart. Generally, when she found Raju enraged, she would never retort to him, even when she knew that he was wrong. Later on, when his temper cooled, she would point out his fault, and he would feel sorry for his act. But on hearing the harsh words, her ego was hurt and she retorted him in the same coin, "If you had married a city bred girl, she would have divorced you during the first week itself. It is because you married an innocent village girl that I am still living with you. I have been fated too, to lead a life with a wild beast like you."

Raju's temper soared sky high, and immediately he got up and slapped her hard. Prema wailed in pain and scurried across to the bedroom and reclined on the bed. Vikram could not understand what was happening around. However, he stood near his mother, wiping the tears with his tiny fingers.

The next day, after leaving a note on the dinning table, Prema left the house along with her son. On seeing her battered condition, her mother was almost in tears. Born as girl, if at all there was any freedom that she enjoyed, it was going to the school and college and this was made possible only by her brother, who intervened with her parents and compelled them to send her to the college. On seeing the mauled condition of his sister, he was filled with pity. Had it been anyone else, he would have combated with him, but being his sister's husband, he was helpless and remained silent without offering his comments.

However, when Prema wished to start home, after two days, he was rather cut up and said, "Well, being an educated girl, I don't have to advise you, as to what is right and wrong. But I personally feel, that it is improper for a man to hit his wife, who is Goddess Lakshmi of the house and hence should be revered. Your husband acted in an insane manner and you should teach him a lesson. Let him lead a lonely life till he feels the absence of you and his son. Give him some time for realizing that it was unseemly to have behaved like that and let him come himself to take you back home. That way, he would never repeat this act in future. On the other hand, if you go back by yourself, he would continue hitting you during each and every dispute you have from time to time."

Prema had never disobeyed her brother. Somehow, she had a feeling that being elder to her, he was prudent enough, compared to her and so, she implicitly followed his advice on all matters. Hence, she decided to stay back.

While Raju kept staring at the setting sun, his mind was cogitating the different people he had come across in his life. First, it was his own father. He remembered that though he was busy throughout the day, during the night, he relaxed in his chair, while his mother sat down on the floor beside him, with a small silver box filled with fresh betel leaves, nuts and lime. Slowly, applying a pinch of white lime on each leaf, she would fold up the betel leaves enclosing a few betel nuts into it and hand it over to him. As she did this task, she would apprise him about the day's happenings and his father would be all ears to her tattling. Though the entire process would require just a few minutes, she would be dawdling around him for hours together. Raju would be lying awake in his bed, listening to their conversation, until he fell asleep. Now, he understood that by listening to her patiently and spending time with her, he was able to keep their love green.

Next, he considered his boss. On that night, when he had apologized to him on behalf of his wife's rude behaviour and informed him that he was on his way to brief him about the tender opening, he had curtly refused to meet him, telling that he was proceeding to his home town for the weekend, to join his wife and children. In spite of his busy schedule, his boss considered his family more important than his job.

And at last, he thought about his Assistant Pradeep. That lousy chap had been bothering him in his house almost everyday. When he did not turn up at his residence continuously for a week, Raju wondered as to what was exactly wrong with him. One day when he asked him about it, Pradeep grinningly said, "Sir, now my wife and daughter have joined me and if I don't reach home early, my wife will take my life out." So, all the while, he had been selfish and to keep off from boredom, he had dropped by his house everyday. But it was he who had wrongly presumed that Pradeep was a diligent worker.

He realized that despite busy lifestyles, men yearned for true love, which could come only from a family. He could have also expressed his love for his wife in many different ways, if only he intended to. But since he never gave it a thought, he was only giving her excuses to be away from home on the grounds of his work.

The sun had set and the place was engulfed with darkness. However, Raju felt that the darkness of his mind was wiped out and everything became clear by the lightness of his mind. Fumbling for the car keys from the drawer, he hastily ran down the steps. Soon, he was dashing his way to bring his wife and son back home, his precious possession.

9

The Spy

For a moment, Chandra was not sure of herself. Her mind was in vacillation as to whether this time she should reveal every thing to her husband or not. Was he going to believe her and give it a serious thought and finally accede to her request ? Or was he going to just brush it off as a trifle ? Or would he assault her for belittling his mother ?

She had indeed tried her best in being a good daughter-in-law and an obedient wife. Somehow, she grew up with a feeling that mothers-in-law were wild beasts, who always tormented their daughters-in-law, considering them as intrusion in the family, someone who snatched away their sons from them. She had also read in the newspapers many times about how the mothers-in-law tortured their daughters-in-law for bringing less dowry or made them work beyond their capacity or about getting their sons remarried if they were unable to deliver a child within a year. One of her friend even advised her to become thick skinned like buffaloes after marriage.

After her marriage Chandra somehow managed to get along with her mother-in-law. Chandra did not mind her shoutings and teasings. She would never retort back to her. Though the ordeal of trying to be nice and calm was unnerving her, she obliged to all the commands of her mother-in-law quietly.

But how could she remain mute to the fact that her mother-in-law was eavesdropping on her bedroom conversation, thus denying her the freedom, to have a heart to heart talk with her husband, during his monthly two day visits from Bangalore. Chandra had suspected even from the beginning that her mother-in-law was overhearing their bedroom conversation ; for it manifested itself in her behaviour and activities. But, at that time she did not wish to complain about her mother-in-law's debase manner, without being very certain. And now when her doubts are confirmed, Chandra was determined to inform her husband about his mother and decided to coerce him to take her also to Bangalore ; for she now didn't want to live in this hell any more. Further, if she continued to keep this matter to herself, she feared that her life would slump very soon. Besides she would also be encouraging her mother-in-law to play a double game, by portraying as best during her son's stay and being her worst after his departure. Gathering up courage, she straightened up on her bed, ready to plunge into him, when he entered the bedroom, after his usual conversation with his mother, before bedtime.

It was hardly a month after her marriage, when one evening, Vijay returned home in a dejected mood.

When Chandra asked him the reason, he silently took out the transfer letter from his pocket and handed it over to her. He was suppose to head a construction project in Bangalore for a period of two years. The first thing that came to her mind after reading the letter was whether she was going to accompany him or not. But, however, she reserved her doubts for a later time, as her mother-in-law was present at that time, and she did not wish to express her anxiety in front of her.

That night, when she was alone with her husband, she put forth the question, which was bothering her since evening, "Am I also coming along with you to Bangalore ?" Vijay wanted to take his wife along with him too, but he feared that his mother would get upset. After all, she had been waiting for such a long time to entrust her household chores to her daughter-in-law and retire in life. He thought up of a plan, which would please both his mother and wife and coolly said, "Well, it would take some time for me to settle there, before I can take you along with me. And of course, my boss has given me the permission to come over to Chennai, during the first week of every month to brief him about the progress of work. This way I get to spend a couple of days with you every month, and we could have a jolly time together. In the meanwhile, you are also free to visit your parents as and when you like, to keep off from boredom." Chandra was satisfied with her husband's suggestion. After all, her younger sister, who was doing final year in college, had always been complaining of loneliness, after her marriage. An opportunity to spend more time with her family, was indeed a matter of happiness. But the fact that she had to remain with her mother-in-law without her husband around, was dreadful.

After seeing her husband off, she returned from the station, and began packing up her baggage to leave for her parent's home. She was wondering, how her mother-in-law was going to react about her leaving. Even before, Chandra could inform her about the decision, her mother-in-law entered the room and said, "It would not be nice, if you visit your parents frequently. Your neighbours would think that you are having problems with your husband and this may also affect your sister's marriage. So, don't go there alone but you may, however, visit them once a month, along with your husband." It was a real shock to Chandra. However, not willing to disobey her and wishing to be in her good books forever, Chandra slowly unpacked.

When Vijay came home the following month, Chandra had a lot to complain about. "I am feeling much bored without you," she drawled. And before she could continue talking, Vijay cut in,"I thought you were having a good time with your parents, but it seems as if your family does not like your intrusion, anymore." He asked sarcastically. Chandra was angry with his scathing remarks and she blurted out, "Your mother has refused to send me out and so I am forced to spend the whole day, either doing work or sleeping. I feel like a prisoner and only God should be kind to me so that I don't turn mad." Vijay never liked to hear complaints and especially about his mother. But, somehow, he controlled his temper and wished to play it safe. He knew that Chandra was speaking so harshly, because she was angry with his mother for not letting her go. And Vijay did not wish to take up the subject with his mother during his stay and create a scene. Instead, he tried to pacify his wife. "Well, had I known that you were here, I would have phoned up to you everyday and saved you from boredom. From now on, every night, you can wait upon my call and we shall chat for sometime, before going to sleep. Also, it is very strange that with a television at home, you are speaking of boredom. There are good mega serials running in all the channels these days, which are worth watching. You could perhaps while away your time in front of the television and I am sure you won't have to kill time anymore." Chandra was convinced and she agreed to do exactly that. She decided to get herself involved in the family serials and enjoy the vicarious pleasures that the television offered. Also the fact that she was going to talk to her husband everyday, elevated her spirits.

But alas ! Once again, Chandra was the victim of her mother-in-law's deceitful act. After having finished all her household chores for the day she entered the hall to watch the television, as advised by her husband. But she was shocked by what she saw. The corner of the hall, where the TV was placed on a stand, was empty and the telephone which was kept over the stand was also not visible anywhere. Chandra peeped into each of the rooms. Seeing her darting around, her mother-in-law spoke up from her bed, "Are you searching for the TV? I have moved it into my room. Nowadays, I don't get sleep in the nights until midnight, so I thought I could watch TV without disturbing anybody, till I fall asleep." Handing out the remote to her, she said, "You can watch it, whenever you feel like." Beside her mother-in-law's bed, she also found the telephone perched on a small stool. But watching television or speaking to her husband with her mother-in-law lingering around was not her cup of tea. Silently, she gave up both the options and preferred sleeping in the afternoons.

Chandra was getting impatient day after day and was counting days, for her husband's return. She was very keen to apprise him about the overbearing way in which her mother-in-law was behaving of late. She thought that this time, after listening to her, Vijay would feel empathy towards her and would surely have a row with his mother and set her right. After all, she dared not to even speak to her. But unfortunately, Chandra had only guessed wrong. For, after hearing her grouches, all that he said was, "Well, why don't you sit with my mother and watch TV ? She is not a witch or a ghost, who would devour you up ? I have enough problems of my own, and don't you try to increase them further, understand ?" Chandra was stunned. She never expected her husband to be so rough to her. Had Vijay been with her, things would have been different. She would have rejoined him, paying back in the same coin. But he was leaving the next day and there was no point in arguing with him during the short period and get into a sulky mood. Controlling her emotions, she quietly went to bed without uttering a word.

A few hours back, when Vijay had arrived from Bangalore, Preetha, their neighbour had come to the house along with her son. It was the boy's eighth birthday, and he distributed chocolates to everyone in the family. It was already past 11 p.m. and just when Vijay was about to switch off the lights, his eyes fell on the two bars of Cadbury chocolates lying on the table. He unwrapped one and thrusting it into his wife's mouth said, "Get cool baby ! There are many women around, suffering in mental anguish more than you do. You know, this lady Preetha, our neighbour, she had been widowed at a very young age. Somehow, she has found a job as Librarian and is taking care of her son single-handedly. Perhaps, you could make friends with her or just go along with her during your leisure time and pick a few good books to read. I strongly believe that books are the best companion." Chandra was a voracious reader and she was happy to learn that her neighbour, whom she had not spoken to even once in the past three months, worked in a library. She agreed to introduce herself and visit the library often.

The next evening, Chandra saw Preetha along with her son, returning home and she decided to have a chat with her. Just then, her mother-in-law, came out in search of her and finding her standing in the veranda, looking in the direction of Preetha's house, spoke in a hushed tone, "Let me inform you that Preetha is not of good type. There is a rumour that she is having an affair with another man now ; though it is hardly a few years since her husband's death. I warn you not to have anything to do with her." It was then that Chandra began to have doubts. Truly, her mother-in-law was no saint or god, who was aware of everything that was passing in her mind. Probably, she was overhearing her conversations that she was having with her husband, in the privacy of her bedroom. That is how she has been able to thwart all her plans from the beginning. She had stopped her from visiting her parents and to watch the television. Nor did she allow her to converse freely with her husband over the phone. And now, she was telling her not to make friends with Preetha, thus denying her to read books. This time when Vijay was advising her to befriend Preetha and become a member of the Library, it was almost a whisper. And the fact that her mother-in-law had known about it, confirmed that she must have secretly heard their conversation, standing close-by. Chandra felt ashamed to be the part of such an indecent family. She had to leave the house at any cost. After all, Vijay is not the only son, who is bound to take care of his mother. His younger brother, who has just finished his college, could also share the responsibility. She felt like being locked up in a jail, with no freedom. Chandra had taken a firm decision. Having made up her mind, she felt relieved and was waiting for the moment when she could break the news to her husband.

From the moment, he arrived, Vijay learnt that something was wrong with his wife. Her behaviour was different and haughty. So when he entered his bedroom, and closed the door behind him, the first thing he asked Chandra was, "Are you uptight over something ?" Chandra was waiting for such a moment and the words burst forth from her mouth. "This time I am also going with you to Bangalore. I have packed up all my belongings. It would be either with you or to my family. I just can't stay here alone, being a victim of your mother's harassments." Vijay was really fed up of her comments about his mother. Every time, he visited her, the topic of discussion between them was nothing but his mother.

His temper grew and even before Chandra could finish her grievances, he interrupted, "What the hell makes you talk so lowly of my mother ?" This time, Chandra decided not to be cowed by his threats and she retorted, "Your mother is an inferior person. She keeps overhearing all the conversation I have with you. I don't even have the freedom to talk freely with my husband. Surely, I don't like to live in this house along with her. If you don't care to take me along with you, I would prefer to live with my family, till you return."

Vijay was now gritting his teeth and said, "Don't you belittle my mother like that, okay ?"

"If you can't face the reality of your mother, then divorce me."

The sharp words infuriated Vijay and he smacked her in the face and said, "I don't like such sassy type of women. Beware of your tongue, and don't talk to me like that again, understand." Chandra was astounded. She had been thinking all the while that her husband was a soft-natured man and now by behaving in such brutal manner, he had exposed the other side of him. Suddenly, she realized that further arguments would invite everybody's attention and so silently, she went to bed. Lying in the bed, she buried her head deep into the pillow, and did not try to stop the incessant tears which flowed from her eyes.

Adjoining their bedroom, in the corner, was a toilet, for the exclusive use of Vijay's mother. Although she knew that overhearing the conversation of the newly married couple was indeed wrong, but if given an opportunity, who would not venture into it ? After all, no one entered that part of the house, which was only meant for her and utilizing the privacy she had daringly attempted to enjoy their conversations – be it their screaming fights or even their passionate reconciliations.

Now, she was unhappy and disturbed by the commotion inside the bedroom and rather felt ashamed that she was the cause of their fight. Her heart began to beat faster. Chandra had requested her son to take her along with him. If her son acceded to it, she wondered what would become of her ? Vijay might perhaps settle down in Bangalore, ignoring and forgetting her and she would very soon be left in paucity of funds. She repented for her dirty act of eavesdropping. It was high time that she stopped meddling with her daughter-in-law's affairs, for her own good. But once again, the curiosity got the better of her. What was her son's decision ? Was he going to leave with his wife ? For one last time, she would wait to know the answer and then once and for all give up the habit. And slowly, resting her head on the wall, she strained her ears to catch any few words of conversation that might throw some light on his decision.

Ten minutes had elapsed. Vijay was shaken by his wild behaviour. He wished to pacify his wife and make amends for his rudeness. He moved closer to her but he realized that she had fallen asleep. Not wanting to disturb her, he draped her with a blanket and decided to complete his report which was due to be submitted the next day. He removed the relevant files from the briefcase and sat down at his table. Suddenly, he remembered that he had left his spectacles on his mother's bed. He gingerly opened the door, so as not to disturb his wife, stepped into the dimly lit hall. He noticed a large shadow at the end of the hall. He walked in that direction, to trace its source. He was horror-struck by what he saw. His mother was standing close to the wall, with her back to him, unaware of his presence. For a moment, he did not know what to do. His wife had indeed been right in accusing his mother like that. Only he did not care to believe her.

Immediately, he made a fast retreat from there, into his room. Somehow, he did not wish to embarrass his mother by catching her red-handed. After getting into his room, he coughed loudly and intentionally for his mother to hear. Then he started rattling the doorknob several times, though it was already opened and once again stepped into the hall. He saw his mother, scurrying across the hall, back to her bedroom. As he watched her flee, escaping like a thief, he felt rather awkward about his mother. For a moment, he controlled his urge to laugh aloud. *Women* ! he thought, *how disgraceful they could be at times.*

It was 4.45 a.m., when the alarm buzzed. Chandra stopped it immediately, so as not to disturb her husband who was in sound sleep. It was mid-December and the religious Tamil month of Marghazi had already commenced. All around, the devotional songs were blaring out from the temples and Chandra got up early for decorating the portico with beautiful rangolis. It was so chill and for a moment she had second thoughts about getting out of bed. But then, she remembered how her mother-in-law had banged the door a few days back, indicating her to wake up, and she did not wish to take a chance again in front of her husband. Reluctantly, she got up and as she turned to leave, she was taken aback by the firm grasp of her husband's hand, who pulled her back to bed. Chandra did not attempt to resist his move and very soon, she snuggled up close to him, feeling relieved in the warmth of his body.

That day, when the dawn broke, Chandra had decided to break the emotional wall that she had erected in her mind, ever since her marriage. She felt emancipated now ; for her husband had promised to take her to Bangalore, along with him. To Vijay, it had been a very arduous task indeed. He had been very prudent while conveying this good news to her, taking all care, about not divulging the truth to his wife, for she would then nag him all his life about his mother's cheap demeanour. He lied to her that he was making up for his rudeness to her, the previous night. To his mother, the convincing pretext he managed to give was that, he was in dire need of home-cooked meals, to avoid his frequent visits to doctor on account of stomach ulcer. Whatever be the case, to Chandra, the moment of joy had arrived. As she was standing in front of her bureau, selecting the clothes she had to take with her, she felt so thrilled, like a five year old in the midst of a gigantic toy shop, confused about which toy to choose. Chandra was at last on her way to freedom ; free from the clutches of the tentacles of the spying octopus – her "Mother-in-Law".

10

The Refreshing Drink

Rahul was on leave for two days. When he turned up at his workplace on Friday, he saw that his in tray was filled with papers. But nothing deterred Rahul and there was not a trace of tension on his face. Relaxedly, he peered into the papers, one after another and sorted them out based on their priority. By evening, he had cleared almost all the papers and his in tray was empty. As he fumbled for the keys in his pockets, to lock up his drawers, Anand, his colleague and a close friend, came towards his table. "Can you spend some time with me today ?" He asked in a hushed tone. Anand had been in a depressed mood for the past few days, and though Rahul had noticed it, he did not wish to break the ice first. Now, looking at the anguish on his face, Rahul at once knew that something was deeply disturbing his friend and so he invited him to his house, to give a patient hearing, cancelling his usual trip to the bar on Friday nights. But Anand quickly retorted, "I just want to accompany you to the bar today. Rahul was shocked. Anand was a teetotaller and many a time had even advised Rahul to abstain from the habit of drinking. He would lecture to him, that drinks gave momentary pleasure and in the long run, it would only cause harm to his health, but Rahul had never paid any attention to his advice, until at last, he got fed up and left him to his fate. And now, when Anand had volunteered to accompany him to the bar, he stared at him warily and said, "Well, if you are desirous to have a drink tonight, you are free to join me right away."

Inside the bar, they sat on corner table. After giving orders to the waiter, he turned to his friend. Noticing that Anand was feeling like a fish out of water at the strange atmosphere prevailing inside the bar, Rahul then asked, "What is it that had made you change your opinion regarding drinks ?"

"Well", he stumbled. "You told me that it soothes the mind and that is why I am here today. I am quite disturbed for the past two weeks because my wife has left me."

Rahul was rather startled to hear this. "But why did she ever have to do this to you ?"

"Actually, it was my behaviour that she could not put up with", he confessed.

As Rahul glared at him anxiously, Anand took a sip of wine and started to narrate the whole incident which had destroyed his peaceful life.

Nandini, his wife was an innocent girl who hailed from Chidambaram, the famous city of temples. Her father was a priest in one of the temples and she was brought up in a religious atmosphere. She was very

God-fearing, firmly believed that the moment you hurt others, God was aware of it instantly, and are bound to be punished for the act. Anand had a tough time, bringing her out of the shell. He tried his best to convert her into a city girl. However, he had no regrets over his marriage, for Nandini was an obedient wife and never raised her voice. She took all out efforts to see that her husband was kept happy in all fronts. Also, he considered her as symbol of luck, for it was after his marriage that he got his promotion, which in turn made him eligible for a housing loan. He had immediately applied for the same and purchased an independent house in Madipakkam, which is in a remote corner of Chennai City.

When Anand had taken her to see the new house, Nandini had almost wept. The house was in a very lonely spot, and there was only a few houses spaced at far intervals from one another. Anand hated to stay in the congested flats, without any privacy and preferred an independent bungalow. Keeping the financial limits in his mind, he had no choice but to buy one in this area, which he believed would develop fast. "How am I going to stay here all alone, the whole day ? There are no houses nearby and you will be away the whole day", she complained. But Anand had cut her short by telling, "Are you not having faith in your God ? Will He desert you in times of danger ?" Nandini then realised that if one has firm faith in God, there is no need to fear about anything. With this belief, she moved into her new home happily.

But very soon, her faith in God was put to test. One Sunday afternoon, it was very hot and Anand was feeling restless. He had just woken up after a long slumber and wished to have a cool drink. He said to his wife, "I am going out to the corner, to drink some coconut water, as my body has got heated up and my eyes are burning too. Just bolt the door inside and I will be back in another fifteen minutes." Nandini bolted the door and returned to her bed, when all of a sudden, she heard the paper hawker, calling out aloud for old newspapers. She had been wanting to dispose off the old newspapers, which had got piled up for quite some time now. She came out and requested him to collect the papers.

The paper man squatted on the verandah and started weighing the papers. Suddenly, a wicked thought crossed his mind. He had seen her husband just leave the house and decided that it would take at least another ten minutes for him to return. He wished to threaten this young girl and flee with all her jewels. He repented that he had no knife or any other sharp instrument to scare her. But then he thought that this timid girl could be frightened by harsh words and as Nandini placed the last bunch of papers in front of him, he stood up and commanded, "Remove that chain from your neck and give it to me immediately ; or I will wring your neck." Nandini protested in fright, "No... Never....you thief." The man then attempted to snatch the chain off her neck, but Nandini swiftly held on to both his hands and forced it off from her. With her fists she punched his face with all her strength, while he struggled to rip off her chain. Through the corner of her eye, she saw her husband darting towards them. Suddenly, Nandini gave out a loud shrill to her husband for help. The man taking the hint, decamped from there, avoiding any further risk of being caught. As Anand, reached the spot, he could make out from her expression that something sinister had happened.

On seeing her husband, Nandini almost swooned over his shoulders, sobbing madly. Anand was rather shocked to see a fresh weal on her right hand, from which blood oozed out continuously. He gave her the first aid box and seating her on the sofa, demanded, "What the hell happened here during my absence ?" Amidst sobs, Nandini enumerated the whole incident. She expected that her husband would be full of praise of her brave act. But Anand only got flared up and shouted, "Does the jewels matter to you more than your own life ? I don't think any other sane woman in your place, would have attempted such a debase act. You must be really having a lot of guts to fight a sturdy man. Perhaps, I should be much careful with you in future." Nandini knew at once, that her husband was being sarcastic. However, she thought that the harsh words emanated due to his love for her and hence did not retaliate. But when Anand did not speak to her freely, like before, she started to have her own doubts. The words her mother had told her once came flooding to her mind. Husbands are really possessive of their wives, so much so that they would not like to see them talking with other men or even look at them, for that matter. She decided to straighten it out with him at the earliest.

The gap between them was widening day after day and Anand continued to remain sulky, though, it was nearly a week after the incident. One day, she sat near him and asked softly, "You seem to be avoiding me these days ; have I done anything that upset you ?" Anand was immediately out with the truth, "Yes ! I did not like the way, you fought that fellow off. You should have been a little sensible and heeded to my words of bolting the doors. Is it for nothing that I have spent a hefty sum reinforcing the doors with iron grills? Have I not been sternly advising you time and again to keep them locked for your own safety ? Being a bit lonely place, I have even warned you several times, not to buy any thing from the hawkers, during my absence. You had not harkened to my words and have consequently suffered because of that !" For the first time, the worst fear came to her mind. Probably, her husband's sarcastic words were directed to her in anger and hate. He disliked her because she happened to touch the man, while trying to shove him off.

Two weeks passed and the weal on her hand had almost healed, but the gap between them could not be bridged. Each and everyday, the sullenness and the silence of her husband, was getting on her nerves and one day, when Anand returned from his office, he found his house locked. He opened the door with his duplicate key and as he entered the hall, he found a white sheet of paper lying on the floor with a note written on it. He began to read :

Darling, I understand that you are trying to avoid me for no fault of mine. When I expected that you would appreciate me for my dareness and courage, you had derided me for touching a man, though it was only for my own protection and safety that I tried to fight him off. I could have indeed given away all the jewels, when the punk demanded it from me, without having risked my life. But these were the ones, that my father purchased after mortgaging his house, and he is still repaying the loan. I just could not think of parting with them. Your sulkiness is too much for me to bear and so I have finally decided to leave, before any thing untoward happens between us. And in case you change your mind over this, and need me, you are welcome.

Anand read the letter carefully over and over again and at last tore it into shreds and hurled it towards the bin. His conscious began pricking him and though he was aware that it was no fault of his wife, he could not digest the fact that another man had touched her, while trying to grab the chain from her neck. This weird character of his, was mainly due to his upbringing. He had grown up in an joint family atmosphere, where the woman of the house hardly left their houses, except on important occasions and never looked up at other men, except their husbands. Now, though his mind was not willing to forgive her, his heart leapt out to her, and he wanted her beside him, for boredom engulfed him beyond relief.

When Anand completed his story, there was a faint smile playing on the lips of Rahul. He emptied his glass of wine and said, "So, my dear friend, though you belong to a modern and civilised world, your thoughts and actions show that you have still not freed yourself from the old and outdated thinkings and beliefs. Well, you have often been advising me not to take drinks, but I never listened to you. And today, you have volunteered, just to ease your mental tension. Perhaps, you have been all the while aware of the fact that a glass of drink soothes the turbulent mind and brings instant peace though the repercussions may be harmful. But have you even once, ventured to ask me why I was going to bar every weekend ? Had it not occurred to you that there might be some underlying cause, which has turned me into a drunkard, from being a teetotaller. This is a very cold and uncaring world, where no one bothers about the problems of others. Now that you have confessed your problem, I would in turn like to confess to you, why I have turned a drunkard."

Rahul lit a cigarette and narrated the pathos hidden in his heart for the past one year. "Well, you may be aware that I was wedded to one of the most beautiful girls and everyone's eyes were on my bride on the wedding day. I prided myself for having got such a nice bride and thanked my stars. The first two months of married life were the happiest one. I imagined that there could be no great a man other than me, who loved his wife so much. While we conversed, I was very particular, to note her likes and dislikes. I was very keen to know the things she preferred and every week, I would buy her a present. Friday night was shopping time and I would take her out and buy her whatever she asked. On that day, it was her birthday, and I had gone to Nalli Silk House to purchase a silk saree for her. When I returned home, it was already 7 p.m., and I wanted to take her to the temple to get blessings of God. As I pressed the calling bell, there was no response."

"Then, I found that the door was bolted form outside and there was no lock on it. I opened the door and ran inside. She was not in. I almost became mad, for I did not know, what exactly was the reason for her absence. Wild thoughts crossed my mind and I ran from one room to another, looking for messages which would relieve me of the tension. And at last, I found it on the kitchen top. The letter was a very long one and I grabbed it and began reading with my heart pounding. When I finished reading the letter, I found that my palpitation of the heart had increased further and I feared that I was going to collapse with a heart attack. Unfortunately, I survived the shock and here I am sitting in front of you." Rahul pulled out a neatly folded letter from his purse and handed it over to his friend, asking him to read it for himself. Anand first hesitated but when his friend coaxed him, he started reading.......

"Dear Mr Rahul, you are a gentleman and it is hard to find a nice person like you in this world. But the time has come for me to reveal a truth, for I don't like to betray you. My marriage with you was under compulsion of my parents. I had been in love with one of my college mates, for two years and one day, he proposed to me. I introduced him to my parents and they readily agreed for the marriage. In between he got a job in the States and so had to leave immediately. He promised my parents that he would return in a year's time and take me along with him after tying the nuptial knot. Since I was only twenty-one years old, my parents agreed to his request and so I waited. However, he had not even bothered to keep in touch with me and two years had passed. My parents were not willing to wait for him. Immediately, they settled my marriage with you and though I protested vehemently, they convinced me that my lover would have got married to some other girl and that is why he had not contacted me. That is how I ended up marrying you, disinterestedly. After marriage with you, I forgot all about my lover and decided to lead my life happily with you. But unfortunately, he returned. He had tracked down my address with great difficulty and come home, to greet me on my birthday and had given proper justifications for his not contacting me for the past two years. Moved by his explanation, I decided to go along with him to the States and by the time this letter is being read by you, I will be flying with him. I am sure, this

would be a shock to you and cause pain to you, but if you put yourself in my shoes, you would rather look at the whole situation in a different angle - how would you like to lead a life with a woman whose mind is filled with the thoughts of another man and just pretends to be married happily to you ?"

Anand folded the letter in the same pattern, and handed over to Rahul. As Rahul tucked it in his shirt pocket, he said, "Well, my wife must be enjoying in the States with her man, and must have forgotten me by now. But, I am not able to forget her. My people had compelled me to get married to some other girl, but the brief and happy life that I had led with her keeps hounding me every moment and I have refused marriage telling them that I need some time to think it over. However, each day, I get up with a feeling, that she would return to me and once again I would start a new life with her. I am prepared to wait for this auspicious moment, even to the end of my life."

Rahul patted Anand on his back, and said, "It seems to me that you do not love your wife so dearly. To you, she is just a piece of wood with no feelings. Had you loved her wholeheartedly, you could not have thought of deserting her, just like that, in spite of her being faultless." He got up and slowly began staggering towards the exit, wishing good night to his friend.

After he left, Anand chuckled to himself. Was Rahul out of sort or has the drink, which he had been consuming for the last half an hour, made him talk like that. What does he mean by still waiting for the girl, who had abandoned him. Surely, he must be out of his senses. As he kept deliberating on the fate of his friend, he felt that his mind was getting very clear and a sudden realisation dawned upon him. There was a man who was willing to accept the woman, who had abandoned him, just because he was still madly in love with her, and here he was a haughty and selfish person, who had not even extended the ordinary human compassion to his wife, which the situation required. After all, she had just tried to protect herself from that hefty robber by hitting on his face, an impulsive act. Well, it is really difficult to ascend to the heights of his magnanimous friend. But at least now, he could change his mind, and give up hatred over his wife. He was now longing to see her and beg her pardon. Gulping down, the last bit of drink, he got up and moved towards the exist. Walking down the corrider, he felt so refreshed and cool. For a moment, he wondered whether it was the effect of the drink. Then he realised quickly that it was not the drink. Probably, it could be the thought of his wife, whom he was going to meet, that was so refreshing.

11

The Grand Fall

Vimala was glaring at the toys that lay scattered in the hall. There were building blocks of different colours which were cluttered on the floor. Her three-year-old son had been playing with them and before leaving for his play school, he had warned her not to disturb the toys so that he could continue his game after returning from the school. Vimala preferred to abide by her son's instructions ; otherwise he would start a tantrum that would turn her mad. Leaving the toys on the floor, she carefully manoeuvred her way to the kitchen and got busy with clearing the kitchen counter which was equally in shambles after the morning cooking was over. While doing the work, she began wondering as to why her best friend Divya had not turned up for the last four days.

She still remembered the day when she first met with Divya. It was on one Friday evening, when Vimala had gone along with her son to the Food World shopping center, for buying the provisions of the month. Her son was standing in front of the shelves and was picking up his favourite biscuits and chocolates from there. Divya, who happened to be there, saw the little boy's hands full of Cadbury chocolates and said, "Don't eat too many chocolates child, your teeth will get decayed." The boy had heard this remark several times from his mother and he was not in a mood to hear the same from a stranger now. He goggled up at her and shouted, "Stupid." On hearing this, Vimala chided him and also begged Divya's pardon. But Divya took it very lightly and said, "I too have two grown-up boys at home and they call me by all sorts of names." Thus began their introduction.

Within a few minutes, Divya was having all the informations regarding Vimala and she promised to visit her whenever time permits. And Vimala was rather astonished when Divya arrived at her residence the next day itself. From that day onwards, they became good friends.

Vimala was reserved person and rarely spoke to anyone. She kept her emotions to herself and never bothered to disclose her feelings to anyone. However, she was an avid reader and thus never felt the need of a companion too. One thing she admired in Divya was that she was always full of pep and embraced every aspect of life with enthusiasm.

Divya tried her best to bring Vimala out of her shell and release her from the coyness. When Divya was around, time flew and there was always a rumble of laughter in the room for she was of a humorous nature and had plenty of jokes to share. Vimala liked her outspoken nature and she found herself slowly opening out her mind to her. She began sharing her views on different topics. Vimala very soon realized the joys of good friendship. How nice, it is to have a friend to whom, one could reveal all the problems and seek solutions.

Divya was ready with tips on cooking, housekeeping, beauty, childcare and fashion. After their friendship, Vimala found life very interesting and she tried to follow her advice on all matters. Her husband was quick to note the transformation in her. He relished the tasty dishes which she prepared using the tips given by her friend. He also appreciated her changed outlook, brought about by her frequent visits to the beauty parlour along with Divya. One day, when Vimala went out with her husband for a walk, he proudly noticed that his wife was wearing high-heels sandals just because Divya had told her that it would make her look tall and beautiful too, and he really cherished her style.

Divya's absence for the last four days kept tugging at her curiosity. Though Vimala tried to contact her over the phone several times, she found it dead. She thought that it was not right on her part to sit at home without bothering about her friend and so she resolved to visit her after finishing her routine work.

On reaching Divya's house, she pressed the doorbell. When the door was opened, she was startled to see Divya's husband with a mop in his hand and with beads of perspiration on his forehead. Vimala was quite shocked, as she never expected him there. Divya told her several times that he was an workaholic and now she wondered what he was doing at home at this odd hour. After greeting her warmly, he directed her to Divya's room. When Vimala entered the room, she saw Divya lying on the bed with a book in her hand. Her right foot was bandaged up to the knee. Her face was haggard and her anguish was palpable. On seeing Vimala, her face lit up. She at once tried to get up and propped herself with a pillow.

Vimala who was shocked to see her friend, yelled, "What has happened to you, my dear ?" This was the question Divya had been tirelessly answering everyone who called upon her for past few days. Concealing her emotions, she explained the same old lie that she had been telling everyone. "I had fallen down in the bathroom last Sunday morning !" But Vimala could not be hoodwinked – for by now, she knew her friend in and out. Also, she was quick to notice the sly simpering smile playing on her lips and immediately she understood that something sinister had happened. She coaxed her friend to tell her in detail as to what exactly happened. It was embarrassing for Divya to tell her the truth but when her friend kept wheedling her over and over again, she decided to let the cat out of the bag.

On the New Year's Day, her husband was watching the TV. He found it difficult to select a particular channel as all of them were airing interesting programmes on the New Year's Eve. With the remote in his hand, he was flipping the button once in three minutes thus enjoying all the programmes for some time. But when he reached one particular channel, he watched the programme spellbound and got excited on what he saw. It was a show meant for couples – a race, wherein the husbands carried their wives on their back and ran very fast. The couple who reached first were declared winners and given a prize. He became very thrilled and called out to his wife to come and view the funny programme. Immediately his two sons, who were meddling with the computer, stopped their game and joined their parents.

Dinesh was commenting on all the men who were struggling to carry their wives on their back. One particular man was trying his level best to get up after his wife sat on his shoulders and before he succeeded in comfortably standing up, the winner of the round was already declared. Dinesh grumbled, why do such couples ever have to join a show without practicing enough at home.

Divya then retorted that even the practiced one could fail in front of the camera because of fear or shyness. At this his elder son was quick to comment, "But papa cannot lift our mummy even at home because she is too hefty." This statement was a slur on his manhood and Dinesh immediately switched off the TV and said, "Come on, guys, see for yourself, whether your dad is strong or not." He stretched out his arms in front of his sons and said, "It is not for nothing that I am doing my exercises regularly." Looking at his wife, he asked, "I may be forty plus but don't I look like a dashing young chap ? I still feel young and energetic."

He challenged his elder son to carry his brother on his back and run while he ran with his wife. But Divya was reluctant to take part in the whole game. She warned her husband not to risk his life but Dinesh was not willing to give up quickly. He pressurized his wife to get ready to see who is stronger, he or his two teenage sons. The boys kept pleading with Divya to take part in the game and finally she had to relent to them.

Their corridor was a very long one and was surrounded by high raised compound wall so that nothing could be visible from outside. Divya locked the gates, to be sure that no one bumped into them while they were deeply absorbed in their fun. Dinesh pulled his wife near him and secretly whispered that if he won in the match, she had to please him in whatever way he wishes and Divya agreed for she was cocksure that her sons are going to be the winners.

Their elder son, Raju was a sturdy thirteen-year-old boy. He lifted his young brother who was five years younger to him, as though he was lifting up a basketball and his younger brother clung to his neck very tightly. Dinesh squatted on the floor and commanded his wife to climb on his back. Divya tried her best to climb on to his back but found herself slipping off. Then, finally when Dinesh frowned at her for the delay, she jumped and sat on his back.

Dinesh was exerting himself to get up but in vain and for a moment, he feared if his children would prove to be right. He then shouted at his wife, "You better start dieting and reduce your weight ; otherwise you would end up with all sorts of old age ailments." Divya was rather perplexed as to why her so far nice husband got crazy and took the whole affair very seriously. Probably, he did not wish to be labeled an old man and wanted to show off to his sons that he was as young and energetic as they were. Her thoughts disturbed her and loosened her grip. She found herself slipping out of his back. Divya was sure that any slip would provoke her hubby further, so she caught hold of his neck tightly. The grip was too much for Dinesh and he slumped flat on the floor and his boys had a hearty laugh together. They once again warned their father not to take a chance and give up.

But Dinesh was not willing to give up that easily. This time, when his wife sat comfortably on his back, he heaved himself to his feet, huffing and puffing. When at last, he stood up, he felt delighted and experienced a unique thrill. Looking at the boys, he said, "If I practice this ritual everyday I am sure to win a gold medal in the Olympic Weightlifting tournament." But right now, it was not the weightlifting game that mattered. He was bothered about reaching the finishing line first, with his wife on his back, otherwise his ego would be hurt.

He shouted at Divya to loosed her grip on his neck as he kept practicing around and she immediately obeyed him. Raju was happily telling his younger brother, "We are going to be the winners and as per dad's promise, we would be having dinner outside tonight and later enjoy the movie too."

The alarm was set and immediately on hearing it shrill, the two teams started. Dinesh was a good sportsman in his school and even now looked much younger for his forty years. With regular exercising, he maintained his robust outlook and health. He started running faster than his sons and was leading them. But as fate would have it, a doormat was on his side of the path and inadvertently, in his anxiety to reach first, he tripped on the doormat and had a great fall. Suddenly, the world turned totally dark for Divya. His sons, happy that they were leading their dad, never turned back in spite of hearing the loud thud and continued to run. On reaching the finishing line, they shouted in great exhilaration.

When they turned back, they were shocked to see their mother whimpering in pain and their father trying in vain to life her up. They joined him and gave a helping hand to lift their mother up. When she finally stood up, she felt a sharp pain in her right foot. She went inside the house limping. Dinesh tried out various home remedies but it was of no use. The next day, she went to the doctor and lied to her that she had slipped off in the bathroom. The doctor after examining her, said that there was a minor fracture. And thus, their New Year Celebration, which had begun as fun, ended in a total disaster.

Dinesh was feeling guilty for his wife. It was due to his insistence that Divya had taken part in the funfair. Since he was responsible for the whole thing, he decided to help her out by taking leave to take care of her till she recovered fully.

As Divya kept narrating the incident, Vimala sat listening intently. Though, she knew it was not right on her part to break into a laughter, but the moment she saw Divya's face, laughter bubbled out of her. She then feigned to be serious by snorting aloud or pushing her hair to tuck it behind her ears or fiddling with her saree pallu.

She wanted to escape from there before a surge of laughter took over her. She gazed at her watch and excused herself by telling that it was time for her son's return and stood up. While leaving, she warned her friend, "In future, don't attempt such things, not even when your hubby compels you. You must thank God, that you escaped with just a minor injury. Sometimes, a small slip leads to lifelong damages, so please take care." With these words, Vimala clambered down the steps, two at a time, muffling the laughter by covering her mouth with an handkerchief and trying her best to keep her mind off from the incident.

That night, while Vimala was rolling out chappatis for dinner, her husband pulled out a chair and sat in front of her with one of his favourite news magazine. Vimala recounted the whole story she had heard and her husband listened with keen interest. After giving a patient hearing, he stood up and approached her. Embracing her, he whispered into her ears, "Now climb on to my back, let me see if I am stronger than your friend's husband or not." Vimala lifted the rolling stick aloft, to beset him, while he ducked himself to safety.

12

The Boss

Moorthy was in the middle of a meeting. His Managing Director was trying to get an important point across to his staff members, who were present in the room, when all of a sudden, his cell phone buzzed. Moorthy was about to disconnect the call, but when he saw that it was from his wife, he changed his mind. Excusing himself, he left the room in a hurry. He told her that he was in an important meeting in which his MD was also present and informed her that he would talk to her after sometime. But Rama did not agree to this and insisted that he should not cut the phone and listen to her. And so in a very urgent voice, Moorthy whispered, "okay, tell me what is the matter quickly, in a nut shell ?" This infuriated Rama and she shouted, "damn with your meeting-weeting and all ! I want you here in just another few minutes! Start and come immediately!" Moorthy pleaded with her, "is it anything urgent Dear? Can't I come after the meeting is over ?" Rama then screamed into the phone, "I am waiting for you at the door step ! Come right away !"

Moorthy had no say in the matter ! To him, his wife was his first Boss and it was his habit of obeying her first, no matter what ! Promising to join her in a short while, he switched off the phone ! He walked straight to his MD and in a hushed tone informed him that his wife was unwell and that he must leave immediately !

Moorthy felt embarrassed that he had to lie to his MD. He thought that sometimes, his wife behaved in a very authoritative and harsh manner, without any consideration for his feelings ! But for all this, he was to blame ! He had once committed a sin ! He had in fact betrayed her and hurt her feelings heartlessly! Now, he firmly believed that the only way by which he could assuage his guilt and atone for his behaviour was to keep her happy by obliging her meekly in all matters and not wound her in any manner! Using this as an advantage, Rama was always bossing over him! To her, Moorthy was like a child and she wanted him to obey her commands without retorting; which he did! He would get down to any level to see smiles on her face! He now wondered, why she was summoning him during the office hours! However, internally, he felt pleased that he was obeying another of her commands!

Though her favourite mid morning serials were running in the T.V., Rama's mind was not on them. She was rather too overwhelmed with joy that she was unable to concentrate on the programmes. She waited in abated breath for her husband's arrival and kept staring at the clock. She was getting rather impatient. First, she would reveal the news to her husband! Then she would break the news to her parents ! Slowly, all her relatives would come to know about it and this very thought filled her with happiness! She remembered all her close relatives one after another! Instead of being a helping hand at the time of distress, how cruelly they had behaved! Instead of comforting her, they had spoken ill of her! Why ? Even her own parents were not understanding and dissuaded her from taking such a drastic decision! They had degraded her so much, without understanding her feelings! And now, all these people who had been against her would be astonished on hearing the news !

It is believed that one cannot change his fate for it is God who chalks out our destinies! Rama had proved against it! If one was persistent in his endeavor and of course with blessings of God, one could change his fate! And that is how Rama became the master of her own destiny ! She can now hold her head high ! God had rewarded her after putting her to harsh tests; for she won his love by enduring every hardship that came on her way silently !

She switched off the TV and sat on the sofa, taking deep breaths to control her excitement! Her deep breaths helped her relax her mind! The memories of her Wedding Day came flooding to her ! To every one, this is a special and unforgettable Day and is considered to be one of the best days in their life ! But to Rama, it was the darkest day of her life ! The past came blooming in front of her eyes. She sat ruminating about the Dark day of her life, five years back..........

Rama was bedecked with a costly silk saree and her neck was fully covered with jewels. She was standing there on the stage, in a very self conscious manner and with a nervous feeling engulfing her ! Various thoughts and emotions crept into her mind and she stood there dreaming about her life after marriage! The pujạri gestured her to sit on the wooden plank. He started reciting the marriage hymns, simultaneously tending the sacred fire by pouring spoons of ghee into it from time to time. He stopped his chanting to inform the people present nearby that the auspicious time for the muhurtham (wedding) was nearing and the bridegroom was to be brought to the stage without further delay ! An elderly man standing there ran to the bridegroom's room to convey the message !

After a few minutes, he returned to inform the alarming news that the bridegroom was missing and not to be seen around. This resulted in pandemonium and people began running helter skelter in search of the bridgegroom, in all possible locations, with the hope of finding him.

Rama sat there fretting to her friend that the garland was too heavy on her neck. Just then, the news that the bridegroom had escaped from the place reached her ears and immediately she got up, taking off the garland from her neck. The world turned topsy turvy and Rama was unable to think coherently !

Rama was off the hinges and she stood there in utter shock with her heart in her mouth ! She saw that, the crowd was slowly making a move towards the exit ! Some of her close relatives who decided to stay for a short while before departing, started indulging in vain conversations. They weaved out stories about the strange and shocking episode on the bridegroom's absconding. With a tear stained face, Rama stood there listening to their different versions! "May be the boy has a girlfriend or something! May be he is not interested in this marriage and was forced to marry the girl !" And still some others were talking heartlessly, "these days, girls have gone bad and lose their virginity before their marriage ! May be the girl is not of a good type! And the bridegroom might have come to know of her affair!" The words pierced Rama's heart like a sharp knife and she could not continue standing there! For one last time, she looked around, wishing fervently that the bridegroom should suddenly pop up from somewhere, and surprise everyone, giving plausible reasons for his absence ! Unfortunately, it was just then that her close kith and kin who went in search of the bridegroom, returned with a dejected face and informed that the bridegroom was no where in the vicinity and that he could not be traced anywhere !

With a painful heart, Rama got down the podium, accompanied by her mother. Unable to bear her daughter's crying, she soothed her! "Be calm Rama! Whatever has happened has happened for your own good! Have faith in God and take it easy ! May be the bridegroom is an eccentric fellow and God has saved you from a wretched marriage! Now try and forget the whole thing as a bad dream and keep your mind cool ! Let us go home and leisurely decide what to do next! If one bad thing has occurred, another good one is sure to follow !"

Rama could not comprehend anything that her mother was trying to justify! This was an ill-omen and she considered herself as an unlucky person ! The fact that all her relatives were speaking ill of her was too much a humiliation for her to bear! Rama sat there crying and cursing God ! Why did He insult her in this manner ? This was one of the most debase manner of punishing a girl, even if she had committed sins in her past life! With all her dreams shattered, she returned home along with her parents, unsure of her future !

Time assuages all sorrows of life ! Besides it also renews the spirit of the victim! No one can destroy the human spirit! And that is how Rama was filled with a new hope! She found a new meaning to her life! The incident turned her into a stone bereft of any feelings! She decided that life has to go on ! One can't die just because of an horrible experience like this! She was determined not to let other people's talk disturb her in any manner and maintained a sullen silence whenever people brought up this topic for discussion ! Also, she refused to offer her comments on this. Sometimes, people could be heartless and their words could kill and Rama did not pay heed to them and let their tongues wag! For she had faced the worst and had nothing to care anymore ! She decided to go back to work!

Two years had flown off! One day, her mother brought up the subject of marriage once again. She told her, "Rama, you cannot wreck your life like this! It is very difficult to lead a life as a single woman ! You are 27 years old and it is high time that you get married to someone! You must try and forget the whole incident that happened to you as a bad dream ! I think that the fellow who ran away without any pangs of conscience, must be a Misogamist and hates marriage! May be it is God's wish to favour you with a much better proposal! Always take everything for good !"

However, Rama was not interested in marriage at all! The weal of the wound left in her heart was still fresh! And she curtly refused telling her mother, "don't ever bring the topic of marriage to me! Leave me in peace and I am not going to marry any one in my life! If I am a burden to you, I shall go and stay in a hostel! Please don't pester me to get married against my will!" And so her parents dropped the matter and let her have her own way! They did not bring up the subject of marriage again!

Though Rama had refused marriage, she could not erase the thought of Moorthy from her mind. At the back of her mind, the question as to why did he ditch her in the last moment kept plugging her ! What made him run away like that? Did he suspect her in anyway ? Or was there another lover in his life? She wished to know the reasons for his betrayal ! She was determined to find out the truth some day !

Very soon, she was blessed with an opportunity for the same! One day, she was buying fruits in a shop, when all of a sudden, her eyes fell on a familiar face. On the wedding day, she had seen him lingering with Moorthy for a long time, till he had escaped from there. On learning about Moorthy's escape, he expressed his disappointment to her and also worried if anything untoward had occurred to him. He was the one who made a frantic search of him and returned with a droopy face on not being able to find him !

Rama introduced herself to him and then asked him the very question that had been bothering her for the last two years regarding his friend's ditching her at the crucial moment. However, he was not of much help to her ! All that he could convey to her was that his friend Moorthy still remained unmarried ! He was leading a stoic life – indifferent to pains and pleasures of life! He also revealed the fact that his friend was not interested in marriage and had agreed for the same only due to his parents' compulsion ; for he wishes to be free of any ties and a committed life ! However, he finally added that Moorthy was feeling guilty for ditching her like that and was wallowing in self pity and always remained crestfallen.!"

Rama could not believe the fact that he was still unmarried. Immediately, she requested him to give Moorthy's phone number and he readily gave it to her. She went to a nearby telephone booth and phoned up to him. When she introduced herself to him, Moorthy was rather shocked as to how she had got his number! Without dwelling upon anything, Rama straightaway expressed her desire to talk to him in person for a few mintues and asked him if he could oblige. It was an embarrassing moment to Moorthy; however, he did not wish to give a negative answer. He agreed to meet her at the location she specified and wondered what it was that she wished to talk about.

The Shiva Temple was crowded and Rama stood right at the entrance, so that Moorthy would not have any difficulty in finding her. She stood there contemplating on how to begin her speech with him. She was in fact nervous and when at last she saw him, she picked up courage and with a bold face walked up towards him. She invited him to sit on a stone bench and sat down beside him. While waiting for him, she had rehearsed several times the set of sentences that she had to begin her conversation with. But on seeing him, words failed her and she sat there dumb not knowing how to start. Finally, she broke the ice, "please tell me, why did you ditch me like that on our wedding day ?"

"I have my own reasons for that !" Moorthy said in a low voice.

"Don't you like me ? Or do you have somebody else in your mind ?"

"Nothing like that !"

"Then, please tell me why did you do like that ? I wish to know the cause for your running away like that!", Rama pleaded.

"Well, I have not revealed this to anybody ; not even my own parents. But I think I will be doing injustice if I don't justify my action of running away on the wedding day. You will then consider me a sinner, for the rest of your life !" Moorthy then narrated his story.

"A few years back, I had gone to visit my friend in a two wheeler. It was in a remote village and while returning back, it was already dark and the highway, was lonely and deserted. Suddenly, I saw a car which was coming at a great speed and before I could move to the other side, it hit me and I fell off the vehicle. Probably the driver was drunk ! There was no one in the vicinity to take me to the hospital. I lay there unconscious for a long time until a passerby who took pity on me rushed me to a hospital after feeling my pulse. The doctor was able to save my life indeed ! But on the day of discharging me, he also revealed a shocking news to me that the accident has left me impotent and that I could not beget any child in the future. On hearing those words, my mind got shattered. However, I felt shy to discuss this with my close friends or even my parents and kept this as a secret.

My parents, who were unaware of this fact, were coaxing me day in and day out that I was Thirty years old and should get married. I refused pointblank without giving any specific reasons. And finally, without even seeking my permission, they had settled the marriage with you. They probably thought that once, I was hooked into marriage, I would silently oblige without protesting. I came to know about this only after my parents had finalised everything with your family. In fact, I had been trying to contact you and tell you that I am not interested in this marriage; but I was unable to do so! Finally on the day of the marriage, I was forced to come to the marriage hall and I relented for I did not want to create a scene. However, the thought that I was spoiling the life of an innocent girl, who might be yearning for a child, filled me with an acute sense of guilt. And when I was alone in the room, changing into the bridegroom's attire, an idea suddenly flashed in my mind ! I stealthily escaped from there and went to my friend's house ! Though at times, I feel sorry for ditching you like that, it gives me a sense of relief at having saved your life !"

Rama sat there bemused. She could not believe what she was hearing! But at the same time a wave of pity swept across her ! And she blurted, "if you think that you have saved my life, you are thinking wrong ! From the moment I saw you, I had been dreaming about the life we would be leading together! I had been considering you as my husband all the while and that is why, even after you ran away, I had been wanting to meet you in person and find out the reason for your ditching me! Though my parents keep advising me to forget the whole incident and marry another man, I curtly refuse by telling that I am no more interested in marriage and asked them to stop talking about the same to me. But I wish to confess the truth to you ! Though, it may seem crazy, I am still thinking of you as my husband and wish to marry you for whatever you are ! Please try and understand me and don't ever say no to me ! And if you refuse, there is no way out for me and I shall lead a unmarried life! For, I just can't think of getting married to another man !"

Moorthy was really amazed and astonished to learn that Rama was still thinking of him as her husband. And he asked, "if that be the case, what would you tell people when they ask you why you don't have a kid ? Won't you feel hurt every time you see a child ?"

Rama knew that he was indeed asking the right question ! But she was in love with him and no matter what, she wanted to wed him. And cooly she said, "I don't mind that and I also don't care about other people! By the way, what if you had concealed this fact from me? I would never have come to know about this ! And what if this accident had occurred after our marriage ? The fact that you had wished good for me makes me forget the whole issue of child and draws me still closer to you !"

That was how Rama had sweet-talked him into marriage. But at home, things were different ! Her parents could not fathom what she was up to and were against her decision. Her mother even wondered if Rama had all of a sudden become insane. And she tried to change her mind by saying, "that fellow had runaway leaving you in the lurch without any concern for your feelings! And why are you trying to open up the old issue now? That man cannot be trusted! For, in the future, if any other problem crops up; instead of solving it, he would simply walk out of your life once again! I don't wish that you must get entangled with such a type of person !"

But Rama was in no way going to listen to her mother! She pleaded, "mother, please understand that I just cannot be happy if I get married to anybody else other than Moorthy ! If I do so, I would be mocked upon by him for the rest of my life on whatever happened to me. I would also have to receive sarcastic comments from time to time. And this would make it impossible for me to enjoy my marital life. That is why, I wish to marry a person, none other than Moorthy !"

This only infuriated her mother and in a rough tone she asked, "and what are you going to tell all the people who pound you with the question as to why he had ditched you ? Are you going to tell them the truth that he is impotent and that he wished to save you from a wretched life of being childless and you have in turn decided to sacrifice your life for his sake by marrying him, for what he is ? I bet none of them who listen to your explanation is going to appreciate your decision and they would only think that you have gone mad suddenly !"

Rama knew that her mother was teasing her and she was by now getting angry with her. "I don't care about other people? Have you forgotten the harsh words that our own relatives spoke on that day ! They suspected my virginity which hurt my feelings more that Moorthy's running away ! They rubbed sand on my sour and today, do I have to care for their opinion or comments! If you are not interested in this marriage, I shall remain a spinster for the rest of my life, but don't ever think that I would get married to some other person !" In spite of all the opposition, she held on to her decision ! And her mother knew that there was no use talking to her! Reluctantly, her parents yielded their assent.

The marriage was a very simple one! It took place in a temple and nobody was invited ! Only their parents were present and they too stood with a grumpy face and their disinterest in this marriage was very much palpable on their dismal faces. When their close relatives learnt about this marriage, they came and shouted at her parents for getting their only daughter married to an impotent man. Her parents only remained silent and justified to them that they had tried their best and were helpless.

After the marriage was over, they set up their new home with much vigour and enthusiasm! The fact that Rama had married him inspite of knowing the truth that he could not give her a child was too much for Moorthy to bear ! At once, he surrendered to Rama wholeheartedly. She was the boss in the family! And whatever she said was obeyed by him implicitly. He was always soft and affable with her and never raised his voice anytime. Like a clockwork toy which starts functioning the moment it is keyed, Moorthy too jumped into action without thinking about its consequences, when his wife requested him to do something ! Her words were law and he simply danced to her tunes. Rama did not regret the fact that they were bereft of child and life went on smoothly. She did not engage any servants to do house work. From dawn to dusk, she kept herself busy by attending to all the chores and treated her husband like a small child fussing over him a lot! Though at times, Moorthy was irked by her over indulgence, he controlled himself and never made a mention of it to her, lest he hurt her feelings !

Six months elapsed by. Her neighbor informed her that they were vacating the house. Within a week, a young couple with their four month baby moved in. That was when the problem started. Rama would stand there by the window and see the mother and child cuddling and hugging each other ; thus whiling away their time happily.

Rama also desired to have a child of her own. Well, she thought ! It is the doctors who have turned down upon them ! After all, they were also human beings! She now wished to trade with God in this matter! God does miracles and she wished to actually see it being performed on them. For this, a strong faith in Him is the thing needed and so she transformed herself into a religious and devout person! She prayed to him fervently that a child must be born to her too! This became a monomania to her! It was her character that whatever she undertakes to do, she would go the whole hog for it. And so, everyday, she went to the nearby temple and offered her prayers! She fasted on Thursdays, not even drinking a drop of water! Once a month, she contributed money for Annadhanam in the temple and the poor people were offered free food ! She also did a lot of charity helping people with money and clothes. She enjoyed doing this work for God and each time she did a good deed, she put forth her request to God that one day, He must bless her with a child !

It was mid summer and the sun was blazing down in the morning itself. But in the evening, suddenly the atmosphere changed. The clouds started gathering and a cool wind was blowing. Within a few minutes, it started to rain. Rama could not believe what was happening and she enjoyed the unusual summer rain ! In fact she stood in the rain for a few minutes experiencing the thrill of rain drops fall over her and drenched herself. But when the drops got heavier, she ran inside the house. She stood near the window, staring at the downpour ! People on the road were walking leisurely, unmindful of the rain. In fact they were enjoying the rain, after the heat. A old man with a white dhoti and shirt was riding in his bicycle! She was indeed witnessing a miracle of God ! The hot weather suddenly changed into a cool one making people forget everything! And now she wondered, when is God going to bring solace in her life ? She pulled up a chair and sat down by the window, deep in contemplation! After an hour, the rain stopped and she saw the same old man return in his bicycle, with a carry bag filled with vegetables. The old man brought to her mind, a Homeopathic Doctor, whom she used to visit very frequently during her childhood and later teenage days ! The old man very much resembled him and she was filled with nostalgia !

She remembered that as a child, whenever she was seized with cold or a bout of cough, her mother would take her to a Homeopathic Doctor. He would give her small and round pills which were white in colour. These pills were sweet and so Rama would take them without any tantrums and she would call him the chocolate doctor. Even during her teen years, when she could not bear the acute menstral pains, her mother took her to him and his pills cured her. Rama could still not understand whether it was the pills or his soft talk that cured her ailments. His advice was the panacea for the sick, who went to him! People who visited him with gloomy faces, would return with confidence and a smile on their faces. He always succeeded in uplifting the spirits and confidence of his patients. He was a very religious and pious man and would daily keep the case sheets of the people who visited him in front of God and pray for their quick recovery ! A crazy thought crossed her mind right now! Why not visit him along with her husband ? After all trial costs nothing !

She told her husband about this and asked him to accompany her to the doctor. Her husband obliged and along with all the reports, they visited him on an auspicious day. The moment Rama went inside, he was able to recognize her and greeted her with a smile. In a hushed tone, she explained everything to the doctor. Then, she unzipped her handbag and took out her husband's reports and shoved it in front of him ! Even without glancing the papers, he shouted, "throw all this away! I don't have anything to do with it !" He then started his lecture and Rama listened to him with rapt attention ! "You are a very young couple and who said that you cannot beget a child ? Even the great God cannot stand on your way ! Impotency is just a state of the mind ! It is a psychic problem ! It is a defect associated more with the mind than the body. How can you decide for yourself that he won't be able to father a child. Sex is associated with the mind ! Don't be in a haste to get a child, for you have the entire life in front of you! Take your own time and keep your mind relaxed and free of inhibitions. One of the best way to relax your mind is to do yoga. Do some breathing exercises to cool your mind !" He then gave a list of aphorosidic foods that are to be taken daily. And then, of course, he also offered vials of white pills for a nominal fee of Rs.50/-. Finally, he told her, "follow my advice and I am sure you are going to come and see me next time with sweets!" And as usual Rama returned with renewed spirit and confidence !

On reaching home, she told her husband that they had to give importance to the advice given by the old doctor. They enrolled themselves in a yoga class underwent training for a week. After that they practiced the mild exercises at home. Besides, Rama included the foods he had prescribed in their daily diet. Moorthy returned home every evening with baskets of fruits and vegetables which they consumed a lot ! A good diet and exercise along with mild pills did wonders to their health! Combined with all these, and with true and unflinching faith in God, Rama was blessed with a miracle!

One fine morning, Rama was feeling out of sorts and was feeling giddy! After Moorthy left for his work, she went to the doctor in the next street. The doctor felt her pulse and wrote out a few tests, which were carried out immediately. And finally, the doctor told her that she was pregnant and her giddiness was due to that only. Rama was too excited to hear this. She embraced the doctor and kissed her for giving the good news. On reaching home, she was restless and wished to share the news with her husband immediately.

Moorthy was very curious to know why Rama had summoned him to come right away! Contemplating on the various reasons, he rang the bell and stood there in great anxiety ! And noticing that the door was not bolted from inside, he stepped in to the hall when he almost bounced on his wife, who was scurrying excitedly towards him! Her face shone radiantly and slowly, she revealed the good news to him.

On hearing that his wife was pregnant, Moorthy let out a squeal of delight ! He could not believe what he was hearing ! His face lit up with a bright smile ! For the first time in several years, he felt like a real man!

With happiness writ large on his face, he held her close to him and said, "It was all because of you Rama! You had helped me in slowly coming out of the shell and removed all my negative feelings I had been carrying!"

"Not really !", Rama said in a singing voice. "If you had not obeyed me in all the matters I had been ordering you to do, nothing would have been possible!"

Shyly, he stroked her cheeks and said, "I believe in the dictum that the Boss is always right and can I ever say no to her !"

They celebrated their parenthood by showering praises on each other for a pretty long time !

13

The Silent Killer

Swarna yawned as she stretched her hands above her head. It was past 10 P.M and she was now getting ready for the last ritual of the day. Slyly, she peeped into the bedroom to check if her husband was already in bed. After confirming the same, she tiptoed to the kitchen and opened the bureau. It was her parents' gift to her for the wedding and she used it to store the surplus utensils and her other personal belongings. Soundlessly, she picked up the rectangular plastic box. It was her medical kit which contained a few painkillers, pain balms and moisturizing creams. She rubbed some cold cream over her hands and tightly closed the lid. Dauntingly, she started looking for the birth control pills. She found that the strips of pills were not there! Swarna was shell shocked and her heart skipped several beats!

No one, not even her husband was aware of the fact that Swarna was taking birth control pills! The fact that it was now missing made her panicky! This meant that somebody had pried into her privacy ! The kitchen was the place, where she spent most of the day, either cleaning up, arranging or cooking. No one intruded into this part of the house; leave alone opening her bureau and meddling with her personal things ! The fact that Swarna was childless even after three years of marriage was a constant matter of worry to all her people, but herself ! Somehow, Swarna felt contended that while she could not control anything that was happening around her, she had absolute power over her pregnancy! For she was not interested in having a baby right now ! Not until her mother-in-law was alive! Hence, every night, she took the birth control pills clandestinely!

She now reassured herself that she might have inadvertently misplaced it somewhere and did not wish to entertain any doubts in her mind! After all, now that her life was filled with tension and confusions, she had completely lost her peace of mind! She was also becoming so absent minded and forgetful! Also, she held the people of the house in high esteem and thought that none were so nosy enough to pry into her private things ! She squatted on the floor, and prayed that she should somehow be able to locate it right away! With her heart pounding against her ribs, she once again embarked on a frantic search ....

The moment her mother broke the news to her that Murali, her would-be husband had purchased a new house and that he was planning to move in there after their marriage, Swarna's joy knew no bounds ! That meant that she won't be facing any problems with her in-laws! However, immediately after her wedding she realized that she had really guessed wrong ! For, her parents-in-law and sister-in-law were just few kilometers away from her residence and both made frequent visits to her place. During week-ends, Swarna was too busy entertaining her guests. However much, she tried to please them, her in-laws were always offering adverse comments on her ! They were making her life miserable and she started to detest their intrusion!

Her mother-in-law kept bossing over her to do things her way and Swarna soon realized that she was a woman who was hard to please. On the other hand, her sister-in-law who was ten years elder to her and had college going children behaved in a very childish manner! These two women on the whole, made her life unhappy ! Her sister-in-law was of the feeling that she had more authority and rights over her brother than her and whenever she was at home, she expected her brother to spend lavishly and satisfy all her needs! If there was a necessity for her or her children to go out shopping during their stay here, she would without any hesitation ask her brother to book for a rental car and would also expect him to foot the bill. Even the expenses incurred for all her purchases were to be borne by her brother.

It was only in her brother's house, that all her friends would come to her mind and she would talk to all of them through his phone for hours together, thus increasing the phone charges every month. Many a time, Swarna had complained about this unjust attitude to her husband. But he only turned a deaf ear to her and once even remarked, "just mind your own business ! Don't bother about the expenses ! It is my look out and I assure you that I will not seek your help in any manner and shall take care of everything!"

Swarna decided to follow his advice! For after this, she did not raise the issue of excessive expenditure of his sister ! However, it often pricked her conscience that her husband was squandering his hard earned money in superfluous expenses!

As soon as her mother-in-law stepped into her house, she would enter the bed room and switch on the aircondition, complaining of the hot weather. During her stay, the AC would run non-stop and Swarna would try her best to control her anger. Once during her stay, Swarna just popped into the bedroom and found that the AC was on while there was no one inside. Immediately, she switched it off !

A few minutes later, when her mother-in-law entered the room, she was rather provoked to find that the AC had been switched off and she started screaming, "who the hell turned off the AC ? In fact I had let it on, so that the room would become cool !" Swarna came out from the kitchen and answered her very softly, "just because no one was inside, I switched it off !" The old woman lost her temper and yelled at her, "your father is not paying the current charges here! Remember, that it is my son who is doing it and don't try to act too smart, understand !" This stirred up all her emotions and Swarna retorted, "your son is now my husband and I have also got some rights over him! I am afraid that you people might turn him penniless! And being his wife, I ought to be concerned about that ! Moreover, if such a thing ever happens, it is me who is going to be affected greatly by his pecuniary plight !" Her mother-in-law did not expect such a rejoinder and this only aggravated her further. She started screaming at Swarna using foul words and this brought in her sister-in-law, who was relaxedly lounging on the sofa with a magazine. Together the women started rebuking her and their heated exchange of words aroused Murali who was fast asleep.

Murali was rather irked by his wife's raised voice! He did not wish to find out the cause of the commotion and silently, dragged her out of the room towards the kitchen. And then he accused her, "I told you several times not to speak so rudely to my people!" Swarna started to explain everything to him, but Murali was in no mood to listen to her. Instead, he only admonished her at the top of his voice, "won't you for heaven's sake quietly attend to your work in the kitchen ?"

It was then that Swarna comprehended the truth! Her husband was always speaking on behalf of his family and was supportive of them ! Like them, he too considered her an outsider in the family and was in no way prepared to listen to her grievances! Slowly, she gave up complaining! She resigned to her fate and put up with their harrassing behaviour !

During the week-ends when her in-laws dropped in, she resorted to an vow of silence ! She quietly did whatever they asked her to do without involving much in their affairs. On these days, she even restricted talking to her husband lest she get into unnecessary tiffs with him. By now, she had also formed an opinion of him that he was not going to listen to her grouches about his family ! She realized that life is nothing but a chain of problems and one has to face them courageously instead of escaping or running away from them! With this belief, she had made herself comfortable in her new home! She valiantly tided over from one crisis to another!

But at times, Fate really tests one's patience and very soon, Swarna was in for another shock ! One day, she overheard her mother-in-law tell her husband, "I am getting old day by day ! When are you going to give me a grandchild ? I shall rear the child like I had raised your sister's two children!" Swarna was curious to know about her husband's view in this regard. From the kitchen, she stopped all her work and strained her ears to listen to his opinion on that ! But Murali remained taciturn and did not give any reply. And Swarna came to her own conclusions! The fact that he remained silent meant that he had accepted whatever she told him. For silence is a sign of acceptance! Or probably her husband who was engrossed with his newspaper, might have even nodded his consent! May be he was willing to part with the child !

This set an alarm in her mind and that is when she decided never to have a child ! For she panicked that if she gave birth to a child, her mother-in-law would take the baby away and bring up the child in her own style. She feared that in that case, the baby would have no love for the mother and instead grow more affectionate with grandparents. Moreover, she reasoned that her sister-in-law was a working woman and hence sought her mother's help in bringing up her children but Swarna was at home and she looked forward to raising her child by herself and did not wish her mother-in-law to interfere !

But how was she to voice her opinion ? Swarna did not wish to make a hue and cry over this matter, either with her husband or her mother-in-law ! Marriage had after all made her a mature woman and she had been tiding over from one crisis to another, without fretting and fuming ! She also knew how to get over from this problem that was blooming large at her ! She decided not to have a child right now ! She was just Twenty Five years old and she could wait for some more years! In order to have a healthy baby, her mind had to be serene ! It was indeed going to take some time for things to fall in line and Swarna was prepared to wait till such time !

In order to gain her end, without as much as a word with her husband, she silently resolved to take the birth control pills. She took pride in the fact, that while she had no control in all other matters, it was upto her to decide when to have a child ; for this solely rested in her hands and no one had a say in this matter!

Three years had passed by! Whenever, his mother brought up the subject of a child, Murali would become so depressed! He wondered why Swarna was not giving him the good news. After all their was no dearth of sex in their relationship and they had been enjoying a happy sexual life! This was a constant matter of worry for Murali! He wished to see a good doctor first and confirm if there was anything wrong with him! He met a few reputed doctors in the city and after carrying out various tests, everyone told him the same thing that he was perfectly all right and there was nothing wrong with his health. And now, doubts began to assail in his mind. Could there be something drastically wrong with his wife ? Before taking her to the doctor for a check-up, he had to first sit down and talk it out with her! He was waiting for an opportunity to break the ice on this matter!

One Sunday morning, after a heavy breakfast, he slouched on the sofa in front of the television. Swarna had gone to the market to purchase some fresh vegetables, as her mother-in-law was there at home and she would expect a feast. Suddenly, Murali felt a sharp pain in his forehead. The pain was so excruciating and unbearable! Immediately, he switched off the television and holding his head, went out in search of some pain balms. He searched his cupboards and found that the bottle of pain balm was empty. He then remembered that his wife had a small medical kit, in her bureau and so expecting to find one in that, he went into the kitchen and started looking for the keys. Within a few minutes, he was successful in tracing the keys !

He opened the bureau and took out the plastic box. After taking out the pain balm, he was about to close it when his eyes fell on a few strips of tablets bound together with a rubber band; lying at the bottom of the box. He lifted the whole lot of tablets and squinted his eyes to read the name on the strips. His mind got shattered when he learnt that his wife was taking birth control pills! He wondered why Swarna was using it in the first place! That too, without his knowledge! He was hanging around in the kitchen, rubbing the balm over his forehead, so that he could obtain an answer from her! But abruptly, he changed his mind! For his mother was sure to overhear their conversation! He then decided to postpone it until bed time, when they would be alone together and when his mother would have also left !

That night, after dinner, he dropped his mother at her residence. As soon as he returned home, he went into the kitchen and asked Swarna to follow him to the bedroom. She promised to join him in a few minutes as she was engaged with the tidying work. Murali leapt on to the bed with a magazine and lay there waiting anxiously for her! Though he was angry with her for cheating him in this manner, he felt happy by the fact that there was no any serious health problem with her! However, he was not prepared to let her scotfree for her disloyality ! It was already half past ten and when Swarna still did not turn up, he got up and slowly walked towards the kitchen........

Swarna's knees ached as she had been squatting on the floor for a long time, searching for the birth pills in all the possible places, where she could have inadvertently placed it. Finally, losing all hope of finding it, she got up slowly ! Suddenly, she saw her husband standing at the entrance with his hands propped on the door. She was horrified and her heart skipped several beats! Immediately, pretending to be busy, she removed the plates from inside and started to stack them once again. "I had asked you to accompany me to the bedroom and what is holding you up for such a long time ?", he yelled at her in a rough voice! His anger was palpable and she started to stammer, "I was just looking for the....," Before she could complete the sentence, Murali moved close to her and shoving the strips of birth control pills in front of her, screamed, "where you looking for this ?" Swarna shuddered for a moment and turned pale! She was torn by a mounting panic and was hardly able to reply to him and she simply stared at him, as though she had seen a ghost!

"Tell me honestly, Swarna ! Weren't you looking for these pills ?", he asked. His face was so ferocious and Swarna dreaded to answer him. But once again, when he repeated his question, Swarna made an attempt to answer him, but the words failed her. Her silence only infuriated him further and holding on to both her arms, he started shaking her back and forth in a mad frenzy. "Tell me why you had let me down so desperately? In fact, you have been killing me day in and day out! You have been a silent killer ! For each month, when you informed me that you were in your periods, my heart would sink! I would then start worrying as to what was wrong with my health ! To tell you the truth, I am really mad of kids and it always baffled me as to why, while we were having a good sexual life, God was not blessing us with a child ! However, I had never thought it befitting to discuss this with you and hence I visited many doctors to find out if anything was wrong with me. After undergoing the various tests, the reply I got from all the doctors was that everything was okay with me and that there was nothing to worry about. That is when doubts began to assail my mind if there could be something wrong with your health ! But I was finding it very delicate to ask you to come to a doctor for a check-up, lest I hurt you in any way. And this morning, by chance, I happened to discover the cause of our not having a child ! And for whatever reason you had resorted to taking the pills, did it not occur to you that you should have first consulted me before taking such a drastic step ?"

The fact that she was caught red handed by her husband was much embarrassing to Swarna ! She knew that she was at fault! She should have in fact discussed about her problems openly with her husband ! But she had always remained reticent and endured every problem that came in her way. If she had spoken to her husband regarding her mother-in-law's intention of rearing the child and explained to him that she was not for it, she could have indeed succeeded in getting her way ! She now realized that she had been so egoistic and self centered that she never once thought it necessary to sit and chat with her husband nor felt it necessary to share her problems with him. She had by herself once formed an opinion of her husband that he was supportive of his family and would blindly abide by whatever they told him to do. Since then, she never tried even once, to change her perception of him. This nonchalant attitude of hers has resulted in this awkward situation ! Though she wished to explain everything to him, she was rather too nervous to speak up. She had never seen him so mad with rage before and she feared if her justification would provoke him further. Her eyes filled with emotions and she started wiping the tears that spilled from it, while Murali stood there staring at her ; expecting a reply from her. Finally, Swarna sniffed and blew her nose. In a very feeble voice that was barely audible, she divulged the facts to him.

The best way to deal with an argument is to avoid it in the first place !. That is what Swarna decided to do. She accepted her fault and sought his forgiveness. "I know that I have done a wrong and I am really sorry about the whole thing ! It is because of your mother that I resorted to this habit of taking birth pills every night. I had realized that you always abide by whatever your mother tells you and would also get irked whenever I tried to complain about her to you ! Though I had gradually got used to her nagging and stopped complaining about that to you, I could not tolerate the fact that she wishes to bring up our child! On the day she discussed this with you, you had remained silent ! Since your sister is a working women, she had to depend on your mother for taking care of her kids, but that is not the case with me! I am at home and have all the time to take care of my kid! However, I did not wish to discuss this subject with you, for I was sure that you were in no way going to listen to me and only oblige your mother ! Hence, I resorted to taking pills so that I could put off having a child !"

Murali was quick to butt in, "and for how long did you plan to take them ? As long as my mother is alive ? I bet she would be hale and healthy for at least another Twenty years! And did you plan to ruin your health and my life by being so stupid ? You are an educated woman and don't you know that taking these pills without doctor's advice could lead to health hazards. Besides, were you not aware of the fact that the sooner a woman has her first baby, the lesser the complications, for both the mother and the child ? Indeed, I have been supportive of my family members because I had all the while been thinking that once a child was born, all problems would come to an end. I have been so much interested in having a child and what made you think that I would part with my child? You have not even bothered to sit down and talk to me about it !

You keep working so hard from dawn to dusk, like a machine without feelings, maintaining a reserved silence, for God knows what ! However, I had not once asked you the reason for your sulkiness and only kept praying God to bless us with a child, for everyone's attention would then be turned on the baby and they would hardly have any time to criticize you ! I also believed that I would then be able to see your cheerful face instead of the morose one ! Though I had at times been aware of their unfairness, I did not wish to start a row with them for that would only bring a bad name to you ! Swarna, you must be a little understanding! It is natural that mothers are possessive of their children ! Was it not this possessive nature of yours that made you take an extreme step ? You did not wish to part with your child, even before it was born ! Then, please try to imagine my mother's feelings of love towards me! It was because of her affection for me that she wanted you to do things in a perfect manner and continue caring for me the same way as she had done all these Thirty years, which was the cause of her nitpicking ! Well, You had always been an enigma to me; for I had never been able to make out as to what exactly is running in your mind! But I really can't blame you for all this! After all, we live on a sphere of extremes and oddities and it is but natural to find strange creatures like you ! And I only seek God's blessings to endow me with a gift of patience and tolerance, to be able to get along with you!"

Swarna smiled despite the gravity of the situation, on hearing his comments. Quickly, she tried to placate his rather tensed mood by telling, "If only, I had had a heart to heart talk with you, these misunderstandings would not have cropped up at all! It was this gap in our communication that had resulted in my cooly taking a decision, without caring for you !"

Thrusting the pills in front of her, he asked, "now tell me what do you plan to do with these pills ?" Grabbing the pills from his hand, she said, "there will be no need for this henceforth !" She then threw it into the dustbin. The fact that she had been knowingly dishonest with her husband had been pricking her conscience ever since she had started taking the pills. Since that loathsome ordeal had now come to an end, she followed her husband, in full earnest, with a clear mind and all set to fulfill their dream of having a child!

14

The Tormentor

Ramaswamy was relaxing in his easy chair in the portico, reading the newspaper, when suddenly a call taxi stopped in front of his house. When he saw Vivek, his son-in-law get down from the car, he dropped his newspaper and ran to invite him. He was sure that Vivek had come to take his daughter back along with him. Ramaswamy was now in a predicament ! Ever since he learnt about the marital problems of his daughter, he was in doldrums ! This morning, his daughter had curtly informed him about her drastic decision that, she was not willing to return to her in-laws' house ! Ramaswamy was embarrassed as to how to convey the news to his son-in-law ! But, he comforted his rather turbulent mind by telling himself that Sudha was his only daughter and he could not force her to leave the house ! His daughter's happiness mattered a lot to him and so without beating about the bush, he divulged the truth to Vivek! "I don't know what has come over my daughter all of a sudden ! She is so obstinate and refuses to accompany you ! I have tried my best in convincing her, but only failed in my attempt! I am really worried and don't know how to solve the problem at hand!" But Vivek took it very lightly and allayed his fears! With a confident smile he told his father-in-law, "there is nothing for you to worry about ! I shall take care of that!" He got up abruptly and walked past him to his wife's room...........

Sudha was brought up by doting parents. Being the only child, she was spoiled by their over protection and always had her way in all the matters. She grew up in a very comfortable atmosphere and never knew what it was to be in need of something! Her parents vied with each other in providing her with whatever she asked for. She had led a carefree life! When Sudha turned Twenty Three, her parents decided to get her married. Vivek was the first person, who came to see her. Sudha liked him at once and told her parents that she was willing to marry him. While she admired him, the fact that he was the eldest among the four siblings and that he lived with his parents and grandparents in a joint family perturbed her !

She expressed her fears to her mother that it was difficult to get along peacefully in a joint family. But her mother dispelled all her fears by telling her that she had herself got married into a joint family and had lead a happy life with her father ! She gave her a piece of advice, "just consider all the members as your own family members and you won't have any problem at all !" The advice had strongly registered in her mind and she stepped in to a large family with full of hopes and with a strong determination to develop a deep bond of love with each member in the family.

Sudha easily adapted to the new life in her in-law's family. Both her mother-in-law and sister-in-law were very kind to her and did not let her do any work. And after great persuasion Sudha was allowed to assist them with the kitchen work. Even her two brother-in-laws were too happy for they had found a good tutor at home itself. In the evenings, Sudha helped them with their studies and the boys got their doubts cleared from her.

While everyone had cheerfully accepted her into the family, Sudha wondered, why her husband was always grouchy with her. Vivek was so irascible and got annoyed very easily. He was also ill tempered and was quick to find fault with whatever she did. And the fact that he was behaving in a normal way with the rest of the family and it was only with her that he was petulant, worried her a lot. It made her doubt if he was compelled to wed her. But she dare not ask him about that !

Vivek expected rather too much from her; so much so that, whenever he was around, Sudha had to be on her toes trying to carry out all his errands immaculately! No matter, how well she did the job, he found a flaw in it ! He would get irksome and frown at her ! And if Sudha ever try to justify or offer an explanation to him, he never bothered to listen to her and was quick to slap her for rejoining! Slowly, she stopped airing her views or opinion to him! She was incensed by his behaviour ! She felt that the treatment he meted out to her, would not be tolerated even by a servant. Life with him was a great torture everyday; for every minute was spent in misery with him. He would either be growling at her or smacking her for something or the other. His mood was so unpredictable and Sudha was filled with a constant fear !

Slowly she realized that she had been married to a tormentor who enjoyed inflicting pain on her ! If she had problems with her in-laws, she could have represented it to her husband and got them solved. But now, it was her own husband who was the main source of her unhappiness ! She did not wish to discuss this with anybody. Somehow, she thought that, when people learnt about their bitter relationship, they would mock at her and also speak scornfully ! She decided to be taciturn and let things take their own course. She was determined to survive everything, for the sake of her loving parents !

After finishing his meals, Vivek generally went to the backyard to wash his hands. During this ritual, he expected his wife to be standing by his side, with a towel in her hand. Any lapse on her part or delay in bringing him a towel would infuriate him. He would start yelling at her with his sharp words, bringing tears to her eyes.

One day, while serving him food, Sudha inadvertently dropped a lump of hot rice over his hand and Vivek fidgeted in pain. Cowering in fright, Sudha begged to be excused. But suddenly he got up and slapped her. "Should you not be more attentive while serving me food ? Where is your mind ?" With a tear stained face, she continued serving him food without speaking another word.

The next day, he was held up in the office and returned home only at 10 P.M. This time, Sudha served him food with much care. However, she once again received a blast from him. He flung the plate away and screamed, "do you want me to eat this cold rice? Didn't it occur to you to keep some food for me in the hot pack?

Go and bring some hot rice immediately! I am famished !" Sudha bent and lifted the plate and after placing it on the table went to the kitchen to arrange for some hot rice!

Vivek had come home very early one evening as his boss was on tour. He sat down in the hall with a magazine and very soon, he was joined by his siblings and parents. The whole family was having a jolly time together and Sudha was busy cleaning up her room. She was really amazed to see her husband chatting and laughing merrily with everyone! Her mind was filled with a speculation ! Was he not interested in this marriage? Was it a forced one ? Why was he behaving indifferently towards her while he enjoyed with his family members! Seeing that her husband was in a lighter mood, she decided to ask him the very question that had been plugging her ever since she got married to him ! For, he had not even once spoken kindly to her ! He was always shouting or hitting her! Sudha was waiting for him with abated breath. Finally, he came in with a morose look and started blaring at her, "haven't you still finished with your cleaning yet ?"

Sudha remained silent and did not reply to his question. However, picking up courage, she slowly began, "just now I saw that you were having a gala time with your family members and the moment you enter our room, you become sulky ! Were you forced to marry me? Don't you like me ?"

Vivek was shell shocked at her daringness! He could not believe for a second, if it was his wife talking to him like that ! Slowly he walked up to her ! Holding her hand, he asked, "what makes you ask me such an idiotic question ?" His look was stern and startled by his sudden change of mood, Sudha tried to play safe by remaining silent. Not getting an quick answer from her, he twisted her hand painfully behind her back and once again repeated, "tell me who is instigating you to talk so rudely to me ?"

Sudha's eyes welled up with tears and she kept writhing in pain and pleaded that he let her free. Instead, he forced her to look at him and demanded for an answer. The tears spilled slowly down her cheeks and amidst sobs she told him, "nobody told me to ask you like that! I saw you having fun with your family members and wondered why you were not behaving with me like that !"

Releasing her from his strong grip, he warned her, "it is none of your business, and don't ever question me regarding what I do, understand !"

But the final blow to her patience was the incident that took place one cold December night, almost six months after her marriage. The servant had not turned up and so Sudha had to assist her mother-in-law by washing all the clothes and cleaning up the vessels. She was rather too tired that night. She stretched herself on the bed to relax for a while till Vivek returned from office. But when Vivek entered the room, he found her asleep. He nudged her and she woke up with a start. Immediately, she went out to set the dining table. After serving him, she decided to skip dinner, for she was feeling out of sorts. All she wanted to do was sprawl on the bed and have a sound sleep. Vivek lay down beside her and started reading a magazine. Later on, he switched off the light and turned towards Sudha.

With hungry hands, he touched her. But Sudha was in no mood to entertain him and with a wry face, she shoved off his hands and said, "please don't disturb me tonight!"

This aroused his anger and he started to rail at her, "what's wrong with you ?"

"Today, I had to do a lot of washing and cleaning as the servant had not turned up ! That is why I am feeling damn tired now !"

Her answer only provoked him further and he said, "women these days, take care of both their office and house work in a planned manner. Despite slogging in the office, they go home and continue working for their family ! Does doing housework ; that too because the servant had not turned up today, leave you so tired ? This only shows your uncaring attitude! Well, in that case, you may go and sleep in the hall so that no one will disturb you there!" He forced her out of the bed and continued with his reading.

Frightened by his rudeness, Sudha stood there beside the bed, not knowing what to do! If she went out, everyone would come to know that she had had some scuffle with her husband. She had all along been striving to put on a false pretense that she was leading a happy life! And she did not wish to give up now ! After a few minutes, her husband fell asleep and she lay down on the chill floor, without even a pillow, curling up her legs. She lay there crying for a long time, until sleep overtook her.

The next morning when Vivek woke up, he found her sleeping on the floor. He prodded her to get up.

She squinted up at him through one eye, and only wished that she could continue to doze for some more time. Sudha could not understand the cause for her giddiness and extreme tiredness. Strange things were happening to her and she at once realized that something was drastically wrong with her body!

That afternoon, she ended up in the hospital with her mother standing close by to her bed. At last, after several tests were taken, her family doctor revealed that she was pregnant. She further advised her mother, that Sudha was frail and weak and she was not to strain during the initial period and had to be very careful! In the night when Vivek went to pick her up, her mother invited him with sweets and also requested him that she wished to keep Sudha with her for a few weeks ; and he readily agreed. The morning sickness was a new experience for Sudha and her parents made a great fuss over their only daughter. She continued staying with her mother, evading a trip to her in-law's house, under one pretext or the other. After nine months of hardship, Sudha finally gave birth to a boy !

While she was happy to see her baby, Sudha was filled with fear to return to her in-law's house. When the baby was one month old, Vivek had come along with his mother to take his wife and son. But once again, Sudha told her parents that she was not willing to accompany him ; for she had not fully recouped from childbirth and wished to prolong her stay for another fortnight. While her father was discussing about this to Vivek, his mother intervened and informed him that he need not worry about this and that she would take good care of Sudha. But Vivek stopped her and gave his consent to his father-in-law.

And now, the D day had at last arrived ! Sudha had in fact woke up very early today. She went and opened the windows and stood there staring into the dark. Far off, a cuckoo kept cooing frantically. Sudha wondered whether it was crying for its mate to join her. And here, she was praying that her mate and life partner should never come to take her back along with him. The whole of last night, she had been in dilemma thinking of her future. The early dawn filled her with a presence of mind and she was sure of the decision to be taken. She did not wish to return with her husband! She had spent six months with him and he had made her life miserable, treating her like a slave. But then, she had silently borne everything because she had been alone then. Now, she had a son to take care of and she was responsible for bringing him into the world. She did not wish to bring him up in an atmosphere of fear and terror. He would then grow up into a coward. She wished that her son must grow up into a brave and courageous boy with a strong will power and all set.to face the storms of life ! That would only remain a dream if she stayed with her husband. She intended to talk about it to her father after breakfast.

When her father heard the whole story, he was almost alarmed ! He remained silent for a long time and finally broke the ice. "My dear girl, you must not forget the fact that we are getting old day after day and who will take care of you, after we pass away ? It is your husband, who is your better half ; who will stay by your side till the end of your life! It is up to you to change him for the better and continue living with him! Things will fall in line sooner or later ! And I also have confidence in you and believe that you will be able to change him faster!"

Sudha was angry with her father! Why was he being so stubborn ? He had relented to everything she had told him as a child and now when she refused to go with her husband who was a tormentor; why was he not amicable towards her! She then shouted at her father, "I had been leading a wretched life with him; ducking and dodging from his frequent blows or the things which he flung across me! He is not my better-half but only my bitter-half and I have taken a firm decision not to accompany him this evening !"

Her father was dumbfounded by his daughter's outburst and he tried to pacify her. "But Sudha, this has been our culture all along! Women have been adjusting with their husbands whether they like them or not, by adjusting to their character, likes and dislikes! If you continue staying with us, won't the society talk ill of you and your parents ?"

His words provoked her so much! She got up with a huff and started screaming at her parents, "father, you are an old timer and belong to the pre-independence era! Those days women put up with everything because they were uneducated and hence were fully dependent on their husbands. But today, things are different! With my education, I know how to look after myself ! It is only foolish of you to advise me to continue with the hellish kind of life under the name of culture! So, please inform my decision to him and also stop coercing me to return along with him! However, if you still do not wish to change your mind and feel that I am a burden to you, please feel free to tell me ! I know how to take care of my son and myself!"

Ramaswamy felt vulnerable! His attempts at convincing his daughter met with failure and he knew for sure that he could not change her mind in anyway! He sat there brooding over the extreme step she was planning to take ! While he appreciated her audacity, he was now perturbed by the fact as to how he was going to convey about her drastic decision to his son-in-law ....

When Vivek entered the room, he saw Sudha sitting on the bed folding the baby's clothes. He quietly sat down beside her. "what is it I am hearing ?", he asked. "Your father just told me that you do not wish to come along with me ? May I know the reason for it?"

Sudha had taken a bold step ! She had decided not to be cowed down by his harsh words or threats henceforth ! Daringly, she answered him, "you are a man of temper and get provoked very easily ! You keep hitting me for each and everything that I do ! Now, with a child to take care, I am sure I will not be able to run to you at every beck and call ! Also, after childbirth, I have become so weak and tired and feel that I cannot take your blows further !" Vivek noticed the gloomy look in her face as she spoke ! Slowly, he pulled her down on his lap and said, "well, if I promise not to hit you again, will you then accompany me ?"

Sudha could not believe what she was hearing ! Was he just trying to cajole her and somehow take her away from here ? For, once she was with him, he could then start his harassment ! Sudha stared at him disbelievingly.

Vivek was aware of whatever was going on in her mind! He knew that she was suspecting him and so he quickly added, "I mean what I say, Sudha ! I shall treat you with dignity and shall not go back on my words!" he said.

Without caring to give him an answer, Sudha wrenched off from his hold and started stacking the clothes in the cupboard. Vivek followed her and grabbed her hand and brought her to the bed once again. "Now sit down and listen to what I have to say!", he commanded. Sudha obeyed him. Vivek then confessed the truth to her !

"Sudha, first of all, I wish to clarify to you that I am not a tormentor or a brutal fellow, as you have been so far believing ! I am a very soft person and I had in fact been feigning like that with you! Actually, an incident that I witnessed before marriage scared me out of my wits and that's why I had to put on a false pretense. A colleague of mine, who also happens to be a close friend of mine, got married last year. Only six months after his marriage, he started having problems with his wife. He would come to office with a despondent face. Being close to me, he would give vent to all his feelings and share his personal grief with me. The cause of his worry, I learnt from him one day, was that his wife was not getting on well with his parents. Everyday, she picked up a quarrel with him as soon as he stepped into the house. Slowly, his problems were increasing day after day and one day he phoned up to me and informed me that he won't be coming to office for a few days. Anxiously, I asked him if he was sick and he told me that his wife had filed for a divorce and he was busy in attending the court hearings! I strictly warned him not to go ahead with this and further promised to meet him that evening. However, my intervention in this matter was futile! I acted as the go between for them and in the evening I met my friend's wife who had by now left him and was staying with her parents. I spoke to her for a long time, emphasizing the fact that my friend was a nice man and it is indeed very hard to get a husband like that. She listened patiently to everything I said and finally informed me that she was willing to cancel the divorce if only he agreed to go along with her, leaving his parents alone. I then conveyed this news to my friend and he only blasted at me. He was in no way prepared to abandon his old parents who were wholly dependent on him. As a mediator, I failed to settle their indifferences and the divorce got through!

Since then, I had been gripped with fear of either losing the people I loved or ending up with a divorce as my friend. Though I knew that it was an irrational fear, I just could not help it and after marriage with you, the fear had become an obsession ! I did not wish that such an incident should ruin my life too! If today, I am well settled in my life; I owe it to my parents and siblings who had sacrificed a lot towards that cause! I would not like to desert them at any cost! Nor was I strong willed like my friend, who opted for the divorce. sI saw to it that you never make any complaint against them! That's why I decided to be your main cause of worry and kept nagging you all the time so that, you won't raise any complaints, if any, against my family members! Also, I tried to torment you continuously so that you would not have any guts to report to me in case you had trouble with any of them! However, I have now realized that all women are not of the same type ! And it has indeed been rightly said that one gets a spouse as per his or her fate and I consider myself lucky for God has given me a marvelous girl like you !"

Sudha was transfixed and she sat there listening to him with rapt attention. She was rather enthralled with his fascinating story ! She gave out a boisterous sigh of relief and then said, "so, your bad humor was all a make-believe! You have been using me as a puppet all these days and I have been timidly dancing to your tunes! In fact, I had been so naive and stupid not to realize your wily nature and the fact that you have been putting on a false pretense with me !"

The dismal look in her face was swiftly replaced by a radiance!

"Finally, I wish to tell you something !" He told her with a grin.

And when Sudha looked at him inquisitively, Vivek came close to her. Nuzzling her, he said, "to be frank with you, I really enjoyed those six months with you ! I liked the meek and submissive nature of yours! I also liked the way you would recoil or whimper like a small girl, whenever I was reprimanding you ! I am surely going to miss all that now !"

Sudha was now feeling very jubilant and her lips broke into a thin smile! Her resentment towards him disappeared like dew on a sunny morning!

"Now, go and pack up! It is time to leave. Everyone is eagerly waiting to see you and the baby!", he said.

Sudha felt her heart soar for the first time ever since her marriage and she ran to tell her parents that she was leaving!

15

The Loving Sister

Kavitha was watering the plants in the garden, when suddenly she saw her sister-in-law enter the house. It was just 4 P.M and Anuradha had returned early from work. For the first time, in two years, since her marriage, Kavitha felt a surge of pity for her sister-in-law. For the past few days, Anu was too much disturbed by the fact that her brother was not talking with her ! Kavitha decided to have a casual chat with her and find out the reasons for her refusal to marry the boy, whom her brother had seen for her ! This was the cause of their rivalry and animosity ! May be, she could sweet-talk with her and find out what was exactly in her mind! Dropping the water pipe on to the ground, Kavitha walked inside the house, straight into her sister-in-law's room..........

The moment Kavitha stepped into this house, she was quick to realize the fact that her sister-in-law was in total shock. Anuradha was doing her final year in College and she was in no mood to welcome her brother's wife, and considered her as an intruder into the family! Anu was of the view that she was now going to share her brother's love and rather even severe his love towards her !

In the beginning, Kavitha had overlooked her behavior thinking that it was her possessiveness towards her brother that made her behave like that. In fact, she even appreciated the love she had for her brother, which was rather very unusual these days ! But gradually, she came to detest her for her childish nature!

During the second week, after marriage, Jagan decided to take Kavitha to Ooty for the honeymoon. Kavitha was busy packing her suitcase, when all of a sudden she heard a clamor in the hall. As she stepped in to the hall, she saw Anu screaming at her brother. "So far, you have not taken me out anywhere! Now, you are taking your wife to Ooty and did not bother to even ask me, if I am also interested in joining you or not! I know for sure, that you have changed a lot after marriage and don't like me at all ! Your attention is now directed towards your wife and you have altogether forgotten me!" After her outburst, she sat down on the sofa and started to cry !

Jagan stood there wondering what to say ! Immediately, his mother came to his rescue and said, "Anu, don't talk so roughly to your brother ! He shall always have a soft corner for you ! After all, you are his loving sister and he is very fond of you ! In fact, you must understand that he is very caring ! You are now doing your final year in college and won't you miss your portions if you take long leave? Once your studies are over, we shall plan another trip to Ooty !" She then began to wipe her tears and this justification subdued Anu's anger!

However, Kavitha was stupefied by her flare-up! Anu was doing her final year in college and was she not aware that married couple required some privacy? Without interceding, she left the hall, wondering if this was the right way of bringing up a girl child ! She was being pampered a lot !

On Kavitha's birthday, Jagan decided to surprise her with a gift. He bought a Meroon color churidhar for rupees eight hundred. Suddenly, he was reminded of his sister and decided to buy one for her too. He selected a Blue color churidhar for her for the same price and happily went home. Immediately on reaching home, he summoned his wife and sister to the hall. He presented his gifts to his sister and wife concomitantly! On her birthdays, Kavitha would generally go out to the temple along with her mother! But she was not used to receiving gifts! And now, when her husband handed her the churidhar telling her that it was her birthday gift, she was very thrilled! She thanked him profusely for his superb selection !

On the other hand, as soon as Anu looked at her churidhar, her face flushed with anger ! She flung the dress on the sofa and turning to her brother, gasped, "don't you know that my favorite color is Meroon? In spite of that, you are giving your wife that pretty color churidhar and bought a dark blue for me! This only shows that your affection towards me is slowly fading day after day ! If truth be told, it is actually being taken away by someone else!" Jagan took it silently, without as much as making any effort on his part to cool her temper !

But to Kavitha, her rebuffs were rather ridiculous! Kavitha had grown up in a totally different atmosphere! Her parents had brought her up in a very rigorous manner! She and her sister were not allowed to even talk or laugh aloud, especially when their father was around. They had no servants at home, and she assisted her mother in all household chores, before going to college ! She had grown up the hard way ! Anu's frequent explosions was something she could not comprehend!

Slowly, she walked up to her sister-in-law and said, "if you want to take my churidhar, you are most welcome to do so! I like both the colors and I won't mind exchanging the same!" Anu was offended by this and she in turn snubbed her, "in that case, you may take both the churidhars for yourself! I don't want any of them!" She then walked briskly to her room and banged the door behind her.

When Jagan entered the room, he saw that Kavitha was disappointed ! He apologized to her on behalf of his sister, "you see, the problem is..... my sister was born ten years after me and hence all of us have spoiled her a lot ! We have all along been in the habit of giving in to her tantrums! In fact, still my parents continue to treat her like a child and she enjoys a royal treatment at home! I once again request you to bear with her reproaches and ill temper!" But Kavitha set at naught his justification of his sister's insolence and was quick to snap at him, "don't you think that it is time that you teach her how to behave! She is a girl and has to very soon get married and step into a different world ! Her marriage will be a success only if she is able to get along with everybody in a smooth manner ! And if she is going to be so fussy, I bet, no one is going to like her for that, nor will they even tolerate her ! She has to be told that her behavior is very childish and she has to get matured very soon! If all of you keep pampering her like this, she will definitely face problems in future! It is high time that she be properly advised! Somebody has to bell the cat!"

Jagan knew that his wife was indeed right and he said, "I have made several attempts before, but that only made her hysterical! She would never tolerate any one who pointed out that she was in the wrong ! She would get very angry and start flinging all the things she got on hand and would create a scene ! My parents would then intervene and shut my mouth and further ask me to leave the place! They would then try and cool her by berating me! I am just helpless and of late have given up on reforming her character !"

Kavitha then silently walked up to her bureau and placed both the churidhars in it, resolving not to touch it again ! Even for her birthday, she wore an old saree and did not wish to wear the one her husband bought for her. Somehow, she never felt like wearing it at all! She feared that, if she ever wore it, unnecessary problems would crop up!

The fact that Jagan did not take her comments about his sister adversely, subdued Kavitha's hatred towards Anu. She knew that everyone were helpless and no one in the family wished to volunteer in transforming her. The taciturn acceptance of his sister's fault had made Kavitha also accept her for whatever she was ! She decided never to get provoked by her mannerisms! Kavitha tried to change her attitude! Afterall it was a matter of time! Once married, she had to leave the house and then Kavitha would be rid of her overbearing sister-in-law! She was prepared to wait till such time without complaining to her husband ! With this changed mind-set of hers, she was able to get along smoothly in the family, without any bickering with Anu !

But very soon, Kavitha realized that her patience was telling upon her health. At times, Anu's behavior enraged her and really got on her nerves ! At such times, she would be fuming inside and hopping around madly without as much as speaking a word to anyone!

As soon as Jagan returned from work, Anu expected that her brother spend some time with her ! Jagan too obliged her and he directly entered his sister's room first. He would sit there and have a chat with her. Anu would then apprise him about her day in college from the moment of her stepping out of the house, to the moment of her return ! Jagan would be all ears to her while Kavitha kept slogging in the kitchen all alone! Though Kavitha did not expect anyone to help her with the chores, she wished that her husband at least spend time with her after his return from work. But unmindful of her, he would keep lingering around with his sister till Kavitha summoned him to have dinner.

Kavitha was unable to endure this ritual of her husband ! However, without grumbling about this, she decided a way out for this situation. She thought it wise to join them during their conversation. Hence, one evening, she took the coffee cup and handed it to her husband. A little later, she entered the room and sat down beside him with her coffee cup and evinced keen interest in their tete-a-tete. However, within a few minutes of her presence in the room, Kavitha noticed the subtle changes that occurred in Anu's face. Her face flushed red and she became restless. Also, she stopped speaking to her brother abruptly. And when she saw that Kavitha made no signs of leaving, she got up and left the room in a huff. Kavitha, suffered this impolite behavior silently ! After this, she stopped intruding and also was determined never to enter her room again !

It was only after dinner that Jagan came to his bed room! This was the only time that Kavitha got to be alone with her husband! And Kavitha eagerly looked forward to this time, when she could have a heart to heart talk with her husband. At times, she even doubted if she was ever married or not! For, she had to suppress all her womanly urges and had to reserve them for the bed time! Also, she could not share her happiness or sorrow with her husband as and when they occurred! In spite of all this, she remained composed and accommodating!

This strong will power and tolerance ensued from her upbringing! Her father had taught her to be an Optimist ! He often advised her that one must see the positive side of everything and not carp at the negative aspect! That is how Kavitha had grown up appreciating the rose in the plant rather than complain about the thorns in it!

Instead of getting worked-up over her sister-in-law's cranky behavior, Kavitha told herself that at least she let her brother free after dinner! She thanked God that Anu did not insist that she wished to sleep with her brother! For, before her marriage, they had been sleeping in different beds in the same room! Kavitha felt delighted about this!

Kavitha accepted the fact that Anu sought her brother's attention whenever she was at home and she brushed aside the same and did not let that bother her ! With this perception, things became easy for her! Also, very soon, Kavitha had got used to her difficult sister-in-law and the days rolled by !

One morning, Kavitha was not well and in spite of getting up early, she was not able to prepare breakfast in time! Anu was getting late for her last examination! When she came to the dining table, Kavitha requested her to wait for a few minutes but Anu was in a hurry! Finally, she left without having breakfast! This infuriated Jagan and he yelled at her for being lethargic! "Can't you get up early and finish your work in time ? After all, you are going to be idling at home the whole day ! You could then sleep or do whatever you wish !" Kavitha was upset by her husband's harsh words! Though he was aware that she was ill, Jagan had been so heartless ! Instead of advising his sister to assist her in preparing breakfast, or at least request her to wait for a few minutes and leave after having breakfast, he just yelled at her, pointing out her faults !

Kavitha became sulky and tried to avoid her husband! While she was serving him breakfast, Jagan noticed that she was sullen ! Though he spoke to her, Kavitha answered him only in monosyllables! And the moment he left the house, Kavitha went to her room, even without having her breakfast and lay down on the bed in deep thought. She had been sacrificing a lot in order to lead a harmonious marital life ! But in spite of all that, she was being blamed for nothing ! Her husband never even once appreciated the efforts she made in tolerating his finicky sister! She wondered when she was going to get salvation for all this ! Tears were streaming from her eyes. She wiped them off and took a magazine that was lying nearby. She started leafing through the pages swiftly when suddenly her eyes fell on the following quotation ! "I believe that somewhere things will get straightened out. There will be a kind voice and healing hands. He will smooth away the fever and bind up the broken heart." Once again, Kavitha's eyes welled up and this time she made no attempt in arresting her tears. She cried for a long time and somehow felt that the words were a consolation from God himself ! Probably, it was a prophecy that all her problems were going to come to an end! Only Kavitha was not sure when exactly was it going to be !

That evening, Jagan came home early. He then told Kavitha that he was taking everyone out and she did not have to cook dinner. Kavitha construed that this gesture on his part was probably to appease her for his rudeness in the morning and also rejoiced at his changed attitude! However her happiness was short lived! For, very soon, she learnt that it was a treat to his sister for her completion of final year examinations!

Anu was now in the look out for a job! Every morning, she scanned the newspapers for suitable advertisements and sent applications to different companies. She attended many interviews and finally succeeded in getting a job. Now that Anu was settled in a job, her mother was constantly reminding Jagan that it was time to get Anu married to a nice man. She further coaxed him to find a suitable bridegroom for her and Jagan promised to do so !

Jagan's colleague Hari, who was also a very close friend of his was nearing Thirty. Hari was a man of few words! His patience was something which appealed to Jagan. For Hari's boss was a short tempered fellow and kept screaming at all his staff. Very often Hari too would be a victim of his temper. However, at such times, Hari maintained his cool and remained unruffled by his outpourings, without retorting, even when he was not in the wrong. And to Jagan it was an enigma as to how he could be so unmoved and take things very lightly! Once when he had asked Hari about this, he replied, "it is what you do that would hurt you and not what others do to you! After all, no one can hurt you without your consent!" Jagan admired him and tried to emulate his way of life ! Now that his mother was pestering him to find a suitable match for his sister, he decided to ask his friend as to why he was not keen on getting married! Somehow, he had a hunch that Hari would be a good match for his sister !

One afternoon, while having lunch with him, he brought up this subject. Hari then informed him that he had an elder sister, who had to be married first. It was only last week that her marriage got settled and since his route was cleared, he was in fact on the look out for a good bride! Jagan was overwhelmed with joy ! He then told him about his own sister whom he was planning to get married and further invited him to his house to see her! Hari was in shock and did not know what reply to give him. Shyly, he accepted his invitation and promised to see her the next evening. Jagan had taken things for granted and believed that his sister would abide by whatever he told her! That is why, even without consulting her, he had called his friend home! The next evening, he wished to surprise his sister and revealed everything to her, "Anu, now go and get ready! One of the smartest and handsome guy is coming to see you today!" On hearing this, Anu was bewildered! However, she controlled her emotions and did not wish to express her shock over this. She dressed for the occasion just to please her brother and agreed to meet his friend. On the following day, when Jagan asked Hari, if he liked his sister, he smiled at him and said, "I do like her! But first, ask your sister if she is interested in this marriage, before proceeding further!" Jagan never felt nor did he think it necessary to ask his sister about his willingness, for he was confident that Anu would abide by whatever he told her and so proudly he replied, "you really don't know about my sister ! She would obey whatever I say her, for she is my loving sister ! In fact, it never even occurred to me that I should seek her opinion on this!" But Hari was adamant and he insisted, "may be, you must talk to her about this ! And if she expresses her willingness to wed me, I have got no say in the matter !" Jagan agreed to do so and that evening, while chatting with his sister, he casually asked her, "by the way, do you like the boy, Anu ? Shall we proceed further in this regard ?" Anu did not give him a reply and pretended to read the newspaper ! Once again he repeated his question, "it is only to you I am talking Anu ! I asked you, if you like the boy or not ?" Anu's face changed grim all of sudden and she said, "I am not interested in getting married right now!"

Jagan was shaken ! He never expected that his sister would give him a negative reply ! Recovering from shock, he asked, "What for? He is such a nice man and

I am sure you will be able to enjoy your life with him! Why do you deny such an opportunity that comes your way ?"

But Anu did not wish to change her mind and she continued, "I don't like to get married right now !" However hard he tried, Jagan could not obtain a firm answer from her and Anu was steadfast in her decision of not getting married right away ! When he realized that it was impossible to change her mind, he got up and left the place in a huff !

Jagan remained crestfallen for a long time! He felt disconsolate that his sister had turned down his proposal and let him down ! He stopped talking to her after that ! He spent the evenings glumly, sitting in front of the T.V. without talking to any one in the family! Kavitha, being aware of the aloofness that he preferred, never tried to disturb him and silently attended to her chores without probing him further ! Though Anu did not bother about this for the first few days, slowly, it worried her! Her conscience pricked her and she wondered why her brother was evading her!

A week passed by in this manner! The gay atmosphere that always prevailed in the house came to an abrupt end! Everyone looked morose! Kavitha decided that it was high time that she intervened and straightened out the things! She wished to patch up the difference of opinion between her husband and his sister ! She was just waiting for an opportunity to talk to her sister-in-law...........

And now seeing her sister-in-law return early from work, Kavitha decided to talk to her and find out what exactly was in her mind ! It was not for nothing that Kavitha had put up with everything in her life ! For she had been very confident that one fine day, all her troubles would be gone ! She knew that the arrogant nature of her sister-in-law would take a sea-change one day. With this hope, she had been silently bearing everything ! And now, she realized that Anu was down in the mouth, and had gotten gentle ! She was sure that Anu would be willing to open out her heart to her ! She opened the door and walked in slowly, with her heart pounding as she was filled with anxiety about the response she was going to get from Anu, whose character was so unpredictable !

Anu realized that her brother was cross with her because she had refused to marry his friend. Her parents too were grumpy and spoke less with her! And on seeing Kavitha who had come to her, in spite of her revulsion towards her, Anu was enthralled! Immediately, she sat up in the bed, and invited her to sit down beside her! Ever since Kavitha had stepped into the family, they had been at loggerheads! For the first time, she felt happy to be talking to her. Finally, Kavitha asked her the very question that was bothering everyone in the family, "Anu, if you don't mind, can you tell me why you have turned down such a good alliance ! Your brother is broken because of that! Surely, there must be some reason for your denial!" Anu decided to reveal the truth and felt that there was no point in further keeping it a secret !

In college, Anu's best friend was Prathiba. Every morning, before going to work, Prathiba's brother dropped her in her college! One day, Prathiba introduced Anu to him. From that day, after dropping his sister in college, he made it a point to speak a few words with Anu too. He became too attached to her and just before the completion of college studies, one fine day, he sent word through his sister, about his love he cherished towards her and wished to know if she was willing to marry him. Anu too secretly adored him but however was scared to give her concurrence without consulting the elders at home. And she simply told her friend that she needed some time to decide about it !

Six months had elapsed since his proposal and every week, Prathibha phoned up to her; just to find out if there was any good news for her brother! And Anu would always answer that she was yet to speak to her family members regarding this! Now, taking this opportunity, Anu confessed everything to Kavitha; for she was sure that she would inform her brother and parents and also try to help her! It was no shocking news for Kavitha and she took the whole affair very lightly! She had in fact suspected something fishy when Anu had refused the marriage proposal of her brother's friend! For no one with a lucid mind would turn down such a good alliance! Kavitha left the place after assuring her that she would talk to her parents and settle her love marriage!

Kavitha had indeed kept her word and very soon was also able to name the day for marriage too! For she had first of all broken the news about Anu's love affair to everyone and then had also been successful in convincing them about the good character of the boy !

Anu was thankful to Kavitha, whose intervention resulted in her getting married to the man she adored! When the day of her departure finally arrived, she happily said goodbye to all her folks and walked out of the family! Anu's parents gave her a send off at the door step itself ; for they had no mind to see their beloved daughter part from them! However, Kavitha and Jagan walked up to the gate to see them off ! Later, they entered into the silent house which was now bereft of the loud chattering voice of Anu !

The whole house was now calm and had a gloomy look about it ! The usual gaiety and joy were missing. She saw that her father-in-law was curled up in bed while her mother-in-law was sitting beside him, shedding copious tears !

Kavitha had all along been waiting for this moment, when she could be free from the interference of her sister-in-law and lead a carefree life ! But when the actual moment of her departure arrived, she was not excited about it at all! In fact, just before the wedding, she had succeeded in winning her sister-in-law's love! For, it was she who had played a great role in convincing everybody at home which resulted in her happy marriage!

It was Jagan who missed her a lot! When Kavitha entered the room, she saw him staring blankly outside the window. And when he turned towards her, she was quick to notice the tears that glistened in his eyes! She then tried to comfort him, "it would take some time for all of us to get used to the change! I myself can feel the lacunae left by her absence!" As Kavitha said this, she felt a lump form in her throat!

16

The Cyber Husband

Neela was standing in front of the mirror, staring at her reflection. She now understood the cause of the burning sensation that she had been experiencing the whole night. For she noticed a dark patch on the left side of her face. She ran her fingers lightly over the scar and flinched a little. Last night, she had provoked her husband to the extreme end and this was the outcome of their argument, which finally ended in assault. Neela had never seen her husband so furious before. But of course, she was instrumental in bringing out his brutal nature that was hidden deep inside him. However, she rationalized to herself that since she happened to be his wife, she had after all done her duty! It was the obligation on the part of a good wife to correct her husband and set him in the right path, whenever he went wayward! She was his better half and hence considered it her responsibility! She did not like to overlook everything by simply closing her eyes to all that was happening around her and pretend that everything was all right in the family! She valued her marital relationship very seriously and did not wish to put up with any set backs !

Slowly, she walked into the kitchen to attend to the morning chores ! The sink was filled with vessels. Generally, she would keep the kitchen counter clean before going to bed. But last night, she had not cared to wash them and now they lay in the sink, all mucky and dried up. She took the wire mesh and forcefully ran it over the soap bar, drawing a thick layer with it. She then started scrubbing the vessels with all her might, giving vent to all her emotions. And as she was cleaning one dish after another, she decided that she was not going to take the first step towards reconciliation with her husband. Her ego would not permit her to do so. He had been very rude to her and if he did not wish to make the first move towards compromise, she was going to remain sulky through out the day and till such time that he wished to make up with her.......

Neela had always been thankful to God ; for He had blessed her with a nice husband. Mahesh was not only handsome but he was intelligent too and held one of the top positions in an IT company. It was rare that beauty and brains go together and when that person also happened to possess a kind heart, one need not even ask. That's why Neela had always considered herself lucky and blessed for getting a husband like Mahesh. It was she who took all decisions for him and he silently nodded to everything that she said.

Mahesh would give his entire salary to her ; for he felt that he was not good in handling money and would not even ask her what she did with it. Of course, Neela was a good homemaker. She did not take advantage of this. After spending a meagre amount for the family, she would wisely invest the balance in fixed deposits. Mahesh was a teetotaller and never had the bad habits of smoking or drinking. He dressed in a simple manner and so his needs were very few. In spite of that, whenever Mahesh was in need of money, he owed an explanation to her ; justifying his needs and only if satisfied, Neela would part with the sum. Many a times, Neela had turned down his requests for money. Once, he had come to her with a proposal of exchanging his cell-phone with the latest one and Neela had explained to him that it was not an urgent requirement and Mahesh had quietly dropped his proposal.

But things don't continue to be the same for long! Changes do occur ; for it is part of life! And it is up to us, to adapt to the changes, for a peaceful life ! But Neela was stubborn and refused to welcome any change in her life ! However, she was put to test one fine day !

Her husband came home excited and told her that he wished to buy a computer. At once, Neela shouted at him, "why do you need a computer at home? Already you are working more than eight hours sitting in front of the PC in your office. And now, do you wish to spend the rest of the evening also with a computer? If you sit in front of the computer continuously, you will end up with Diabetes and various other ailments due to your sedentary lifestyle! I won't let you buy one ! Moreover, who has that much money for it ? All the money we have are tied up with the banks as fixed deposits and right now, I don't have any money on hand!" But Mahesh continued to pacify and cajole her, "my dear, you don't have to shell out any money for that ! My office is giving interest free loan to buy a PC and everyone is going for it and that is why I too wish to utilize the opportunity !" Though Neela was surprised by her husband's obduracy, she gave in without disputing.

Once the PC came in to the house, Mahesh got an internet connection immediately. That is when the actual problem started for Neela. For, the moment he returned from office, he would change his clothes and go and sit in front of the PC and start browsing. He would keep himself busy till late night. For the first few days, Neela did not comment on this. She thought that he was probably busy with some project work and let him do his job without disturbing him.

However, the fact the he did not spend time with his three year old son worried her. Whenever the little boy approached him, he simply pushed him off with the words, "don't disturb daddy now ; go and play with mummy !" The little boy after standing beside him for a while with a droopy face, would trot back to his mother and start pestering her for something or the other. Neela was irked by this fact !

More than this, she felt bad that Mahesh did not spend much time with her. Generally, he would keep lingering with her in the kitchen. He would keep tweaking or cuddling her from time to time while Neela would keep shoving him off telling him that she was busy ; while really she enjoyed it. All that fun was missing in her life now since the arrival of the computer, as Mahesh was always glued to his PC and did not let any one near him. At times, Mahesh would even help her with the dinner, but now he did not even enter the kitchen. And whenever Neela went up to him and sat down for a chat, he became restless and asked her not to perturb him.

One evening, Neela went to him with his coffee cup and found that he had gone to the toilet. She placed it on his table and by chance happened to glance at the PC screen. She was shocked to see sexy photos of women on the screen. She felt a sudden jolt in her stomach and it is only now that everything became crystal clear to her. That is why he was rather irked whenever she went near him. Silently, she returned without talking to him about this.

The next day, while her husband was away to the office, she switched on the PC and opened up the sites her husband had been browsing the previous night. She was almost alarmed and wished to shriek aloud. He had been indulging in chatting in the internet with women. Not only that ! He had been discussing about sex with these women !

Neela was sullen and dismal for the rest of the day. Why did her husband behave in this manner ? After all, she loved her husband so much and pleased him very much in bed. There was no dearth of sex in his life. Even at times, when she had been too tired or unwell, she had never complained about it to him when he came to her with the intention of having sex. Why then, his mind was going haywire and he was becoming a sex addict that to in the internet. She had to put a stop to this and wished to talk it out with her husband very soon !

That evening, as usual Mahesh was busy engaged in chatting with a woman on sex and slyly Neela stood by his side watching him, keying in the words. He had been so much engrossed with his chatting that he was not aware that his wife was standing beside him and examining his work. He was shamelessly discussing about his personal sex life with some unknown woman. Neela felt ashamed of him. She placed the coffee cup on the table with a loud thud, spilling some coffee on the table in the process and sat down in front of him. Mahesh continued with his chatting without acknowledging her presence ; nor did he comment about the spilled coffee. Her son was sleeping and she knew that this was the right time to discuss everything with her husband!

"Can I have a frank talk with you for a few minutes please ?" She asked in a gruffy voice.

Mahesh stopped his work and turned to her. "Yes Madam, you are most welcome to do so !"

"Why have you been cheating me all these days?", She asked with a sad face. "You told me that you are busy browsing for some information to complete your project work but I now found out what exactly you are doing ! You are engaged in ignoble chatting with some unknown women about sex ! In fact, I feel very mortified about it ! I don't like it and I want you to stop doing this hence forth !"

The fact that his wife was aware of what he was doing was embarrassing to him! But without expressing his distress, he told her, "so what Neela? Why are you so upset over this? This is cyber age and I am just chatting with some unknown women and that too for fun ! I am not going to touch them nor do I plan to run away along with them! What is wrong in it? You seem to be so worked up over nothing at all!"

But Neela could not be easily convinced and she asked, "what if that woman happens to be some one next door ! Won't you get into problems then ?"

Mahesh laughed aloud! "No way Neela! Our women ; that to women from Chennai are not that brave enough to have such conversations and please stop imagining wild things !"

Once again, she pleaded with him, "why are you being so mulish this time ! Why don't you listen to me? I don't like you to chat with any of the women, and won't you stop it for my sake !"

At last, Mahesh stood up. "O.K Dear ! I shall stop it right away !" He turned off the computer and accompanied her to the kitchen.

Mahesh sat there in the kitchen with a grumpy face as he was not able to continue his chatting in the internet. Neela was quick to notice his sulkiness and she continued her lecture once again! "You know something! The internet is packed with lot of information and the overload of information only makes your mind blank ! I have read some time back that in Philipines, internet has become an addiction and is affecting the lives and families of many. Young teenagers are addicted to the computer round the clock! They keep browsing pronographic sites and enjoy cyber sex. They are so much obsessed with the online world and such cyberspace contact only results in mental disorders. I was surprised to learn that in that country, there are also internet hospitals where teenage children who are obsessed with the internet and suffer from mental problems are taken for treatment ! Your obsession with internet has resulted in neglect of real life personal relationships. You don't interact with me like before and hardly care for your son and me these days! You also disregard your health by not getting good sleep and your eyes are looking dull! In fact, you are also struck with online marital infidelity and if you don't stop it now, I think you would end up in trouble !"

Mahesh listened to her without retorting. Finally he mocked at her, "you must have gone as a lecturer to some college, Neela ! Your students would have probably enjoyed listening to you ! You read a lot and keep yourself abreast with the latest news ! Unfortunately, here I am, trapped by your side and is forced to listen to your lectures from time to time !"

Neela was rejoicing in the fact that she was able to convince her husband! But her happiness was short lived! For the next evening, when he returned from office, he went and sat before the computer, as usual. He did not even care to lift his son, who came happily running after him.

Neela was dumbfounded ! She was by now sure that her husband had become a cyber addict. He behaved like an alcoholic who keeps promising that he would quit drinking after one more drink. She came up to him and placed the coffee cup with a thud on his table and stood in front of him with her hands on her hips. Mahesh was in the midst of an interesting chatting session and he did not care a fig for her rude behaviour. This provoked her and immediately, she came near him and yelled, "are you going to stop this or not ?"

"Just leave me alone for another half another ! I shall join you after that !", he told her, without lifting his head from the computer.

Neela's anger rose higher ! She leaped in front of him and switched off the computer. Mahesh was annoyed with this. But he controlled his temper and calmly took a sip of the coffee. He then grabbed her arm and pulled her out of his room. After that, he once again switched on the PC and started logging on to his website. Neela was adamant and she decided not to let him have his way ! She was determined to fight out to the end, no matter what ! She returned once again, and switched off the PC and Mahesh was helpless ! Angrily he asked, "what has come over you today ? You are behaving like a crazy child ! Now, get out from here right away !" When he tried to restart the computer again, Neela pulled out the wires thus disabling the connection ! Unable to bear with her atrocious behavior, Mahesh slapped her. Neela was stunned. Her eyes filled up with tears. "How dare you hit me like this ! You brute ! See, the internet has made you mad already ! You have never hit me before and it is your madness which makes you act like this !"

"It is you who is behaving in a hysterical manner, Neela ! Can't you just leave me alone for a while ? Now, are you going to leave the place or not ?"

The fact that he had hit her got on her nerves and she once again swiftly pulled out the mouse and flung it across the room. Provoked by this, Mahesh slapped her once again ; this time, harder than before. With tears streaming from her eyes, she said, "don't you have any feelings towards me ? I keep telling you to stop this browsing and chatting business and you hardly pay attention to me ! And now you started hitting me as if I were your slave ! You will never be able to use the computer again !" She said and started lifting the computer. Mustering up all her strength and courage, she lifted the computer. Even before Mahesh could do anything to stop her, she dropped it on to the floor dauntlessly. For a few seconds, Mahesh became speechless at his wife's outrage ! The computer lay shattered to pieces. Mahesh was fuming inside on seeing the total wreck before his eyes. Gnashing his teeth, he was urgently looking around for something to hit her with. Suddenly, his eyes fell on the steaming coffee cup. He took it and splashed the hot coffee over her face. Neela squirmed in great pain. Screaming aloud, she ran to her bedroom, while her son ran behind her crying.

Mahesh stood there for long, examining the broken pieces of the computer and realized that it was beyond repair. He pushed the parts towards the dusbin with his foot. His mind was turbulent. While he felt sorry for acting so wildly with his wife, he also felt bad that she had shattered his new computer, the loan amount of which was still due. Silently, he went to the hall and switched on the television.

When his mind became relaxed, he got up and went to the bedroom. He saw that Neela was already asleep, and his little son was huddled close to her with wide open eyes. But on seeing him, he immediately squeezed them shut and pretended to be asleep ; for he dare not see his father. Mahesh switched off the light and lay down by his side without speaking a word........

And now, as Neela was cleaning the vessels, she kept ruminating over last night's incident. She was indeed aware of the fact that she was also at fault; for she had smashed a brand new and expensive computer! This would of course make any one furious! But then, she rationalized that if she had not done so, her husband would have surely become an internet addict. She did not want him to be a cyber husband, one who was always peering into a PC ! She wished to regain his attention and love ; which of late was turned towards other women. Though it was only through chatting in the internet, she could not tolerate that ! Surely, this would in the long run affect both his mind and body ! Her drastic step to destroy the computer once and for all was the only way out ! She was happy that she was able to nip this habit in the bud itself, which was standing in the way of their otherwise smooth marital relationship ! May be, she thought, she must not repent for it again !

Her reasoning thoughts were disturbed by her husband's loud voice. "Where is my coffee?" He screamed standing at the entrance of the kitchen.

"the milk has to boil !" She said, even without looking up at him.

"Is Madam so busy that she can't bring my bed coffee in time ? Do I have to come here begging for it?"

Neela slowly turned back and started stacking the vessels in the cupboard, without giving him a reply. Suddenly, the dark scar on her face caught his eye. He looked at her momentarily in shock. Slowly, he walked up to her. Holding her chin with his hand, he examined it closely and yelled, "what the hell is this?"

Shoving off his hand from her face, Neela shot back, "it is all due to your madness ! Didn't you pour hot coffee over my face last night ?" He watched her face with love in his eyes. He knew that the wound caused by his rough behavior must have been too painful for her. Mahesh was filled with remorse! Suddenly, he softened towards her. In a feeble tone, he said, "but did you not behave like one too? My God! I still wonder, where you got all that energy from to be able to lift the computer and drop it down like that! I don't think, even an ace technician will be able to rectify it ! It has got shattered to pieces! I have put it near the dustbin ! Don't forget to clear it off ! Neela felt elated and there was a gleam of victory in her eyes! Her fight to the finish to get rid of the computer that brought chaos into her life, ended successfully. Despite the pain, Neela found herself quivering with laughter !

17

A Leap in the Dark

Lakshmi took out the letter from the drawer and started reading it once again! She was reading it for the umpteenth time, since this morning. It was from her only son living in the States. The letter was a bolt from the blue; for each time Lakshmi read it, she became dumbfounded and tears rolled down from her eyes. She could not believe that her son, the only soul on earth, who gave meaning to her life was deserting her ! Suddenly, Lakshmi felt utterly lost in this world!

Her neighbours had warned her that, once children are sent to America, they hardly have mind to return! They get carried away by the different lifestyle prevailing there and most of them acquire the country's citizenship and once and for all settle there. To emphasize their point and convince her, they had even sited examples of young men, who left the house with a promise of enriching the family, but instead got married and forgot their own families. They had told her that since her husband had left enough money to take care of her for the rest of her life, she need not have to send her only son to America. Now that her son had finished his Engineering Degree, she could get him married and enjoy her life with her grandchildren. But Lakshmi did not listen to them !

Not that Lakshmi wished to lead a lonely life! But she had in fact no control over taking any decision in this matter ! Her son was very adamant and was pleading with her to change her mind ! He cajoled her that he was going to be away for just two years and once his contract was over, he would return to India and get married to the girl of her choice. Further, he brainwashed her that his US experience would increase his job opportunities in India. Lakshmi had no other go, but to accede to his request! Each time, he phoned up to her, she complained to him that she was feeling lonely and bored !

Two years had flown by quickly! Now, she was eagerly waiting for her son's arrival! But this morning, she got a letter from her son. Anxiously, she tore open the letter and started to read its content. She was flabbergasted! He informed her that due to some unforeseen circumstances, he was compelled to get married to an American girl. And when he had requested her to accompany him to India, the girl refused and he did not have mind to leave her either. So he has decided to settle down in the States. However, he promised to visit her next year and stay with her for a month. Right now, he was busy with some new assignment and would not be able to come to India. She realised that her son did not belong to her any more ! She had lost him for ever !

Lakshmi sobbed for a long time ! Finally, she wiped away her tears! She took a drastic decision ! She was not going to let this shatter her life! She was only Forty Five years old! And Fate had dealt her one blow after another! Failures and shocks were nothing new to her ! She had faced all the blows of fate single-handedly without complaining ! And now, she was sure that she could get over this too ! Afterall, time assuages everything ! She did not wish to spend the rest of her life wallowing in self pity. She decided let by gones be by gones and let God's will be done ! Life on earth is worthy only if we have somebody to love and care for or atleast have someone who would love and care for us! Otherwise, it would have no value at all ! She knew how to bring back meaning to her life! She stood up, bursting with a new confidence. She bolted the doors, not only of her house, but to the whole world as well and walked briskly towards the temple. She knew that Krishnan, her newly acquired Friend, Philosopher and Guide would eagerly be waiting for her arrival in the temple. She wished to talk it out with him! She had at last decided to give in to his proposal ; for he was also like her, dying for a companion in life. After all, if God shuts one door, he also opens another and it is only upto us to make use of it.

Lakshmi had been the youngest of three daughters. She was born in a family, where fun, laughter and gossip were the watchword. But when her father got her married to a rich businessman living in Chennai City, her life changed completely. It was then that she started to experience failures in life, one after another. Her husband was a workholic and was always very busy. Finding her husband always busy and away on tours, she dreamed of starting a family and desired to have many children. But it was with great difficulty, after running from one doctor to another and a period of almost eight years that she was gifted with only one son. Many a time, Lakshmi had warned her husband to slow down his pace of working as there was no dearth of money and he could now spend more time with his son and her. But he hardly paid any attention to her advice. And one morning, his hard work and toil took a toll on his life. He died of an heart-attack! Now she turned to her only son, who was studying in Plus Two, for solace. She had been dreaming that one day, her son would grow up and take loving care of her in her old age. She would then have grandchildren whom she could enjoy her life with. But after completion of his Engineering Degree, her son had got an offer for working in States and he pleaded with his mother that he wished to take up this assignment for just a period of two years and promised to return to India after completion of his contract. Lakshmi agreed to his request for she trusted her son.

In order to beat boredom, Lakshmi started to go to the nearby temple. One day, while coming round the Temple, she was deeply pained by the loneliness she was experiencing in her life. She cursed God for taking away her husband at a time, when he had promised her that he would slow down a little in his business activity. Suddenly her BP soared very high and engulfed by a bout of giddiness, she fainted. Krishnan was just walking behind her. He stood aside for a while. None of the women folks who were walking past her, cared to stop by and lift her up. Finally, Krishnan fetched some water and offered it to her. When at last, she sat up, he asked her,"what happened?"

"I have B.P. and suddenly it has shot up, that is all !" , Lakshmi said, heaving herself up. Krishnan held her arm and helped her to her feet. Slowly, he led her to the nearby platform and asked her to rest for a while before leaving the temple. Lakshmi reclined on the pillar close by. Krishnan continued to linger around for some time. Observing that she was still feeling tired, he asked, "are you O.K. now ? Or shall I accompany you to your house ?"

"Thanks for all the help ! I am alright now and you don't have to bother !" she said.

When the twilight turned to dusk, Lakshmi left the temple. She entered the desolate house which was depressingly silent. That night, as she went to bed, she could not sleep. She thought of the stranger who lent a helping hand to her ! Somehow, she felt that she had not thanked him enough ! And if she chanced to meet him again, she wished to express her gratitude to him once again. She was lucky ; for she was able to meet him the next day in the temple. When she went and stood in front of him, Krishnan was quick to recognize her. While she started appreciating his kind gesture, he cut in sharply, "could you not bring somebody with you ? Why did you come alone ?"

Taken aback by his rudeness, she shot back, "I don't have anybody ! I am staying alone ! My husband is no more and my only son is living in States !"

Krishnan could not believe what he was hearing ! He felt sorry that he had shouted at her like that and apologized to her immediately. She sat down and told him her story. Krishnan too listened patiently, all the while peering into her eyes ! For he had all the time in this world !

That was how their acquaintance began two years back! From then on, Lakshmi met him in the temple everyday. She found that Krishnan was a congenial and loquacious person. He was a compulsive talker and kept plugging her with questions one after another. Very soon Lakshmi realised that, Krishnan was also sailing in the same boat as hers ! Like her, he was also visiting the temple for killing time and his mind was also filled with grief ! After his daughter's marriage was over, Krishnan decided to take voluntary retirement from his service. He and his wife decided to go for a walk every morning to keep themselves in good health and fitness. One fine morning, as they were returning from their walk, a car, whose driver was rather drunk, knocked his wife! Krishnan saw his wife float high up in the air screaming and fall dead to the ground in front of his eyes ! His dreams of a happy retired life got shattered. He mourned her death for almost three years and only now he started coming out of the shell. He visited the temple every evening, just to spend his time! On learning from Lakshmi that she had also lost her husband and was living all alone, he spoke to her lovingly. Everyday, he would enquire her about her health and if her son had written to her. And on days, when Lakshmi did not turn up at the temple, he would visit her house, just to find out if everything was o.k with her. His visits set the tongues of women in the neighbourhood wagging. On one occasion, when she had gone up to the gate to see him off, she overheard two women talking behind her, "look at these two people. At this age, they are making love! They assume themselves to be adolescents!

Things have gone worse these days! How can one expect rain in Chennai with such people around !"

Lakshmi silently entered her house without caring for their remarks. Afterall, what they were saying was quite true! At times, she herself felt bad for straying from the right path! But then, the ways of the mind are unpredictable! No one knows for sure, where it would lead us on ! She justified that, probably if they were in her shoes, they would also do the same thing ! For how long could one remain all alone, without any companion to talk to at home! Lakshmi was really feeling young at heart for a strong feeling of love and understanding began to grow between them. They could not remain even for a day without meeting each other. They looked forward to their temple meetings with great enthusiasm! For they had much to confide in each other and share their grief. At times, Lakshmi cooked special dishes for him and brought it to the temple ! Once, while relishing her tamarind rice, he said, "why don't you come home and stay with me ! I am nearing fifty and finding it very difficult to do all the cooking and house work. May be, if you stayed with me, we can share the work! Both of us don't have anybody waiting for us back home! Sometimes, it pains a lot to enter the empty house, which is so gloomy ! And on days, when I don't see you in the temple, I get worried that something has happened to you and I have to come rushing to your house! If we stay together, we can be of assistance to each other and that will also help us in ageing peacefully!

The loving and caring words were indeed pleasing to her ears! But Lakshmi did not like to be drawn into this relationship. And immediately she said, "well, if my not turning up to the temple bothers you a lot, I shall make it a point to visit regularly henceforth and listen to your talk! But right now I am expecting my son to return from the States! He may arrive anytime as his two years period has elapsed already ! I am planning to get him married and spend the rest of my life with my grandchildren ! You don't have to worry about me, for once my son returns, he would take loving care of me!"

Krishnan listened to her patiently. Then with a smile on his face, he said, "that's fine ! But what if I don't be able to come to the temple continuously, due to some sickness !"

"In that case, I shall come and see you without fail !" she retorted.

After that Krishnan did not press her to change her mind! He felt contented to just see her every evening in the temple !

And now Lakshmi was once again betrayed by God! She had been all the while hoping that her son would return and her new life would begin! But things turned topsy turvy! From her son's letter, she understood that, he was planning to ditch her ! Well, she thought! With her son having married a US girl, surely he would never return to India and settle down with her. Lakshmi realised that she had lost her son for ever! She had faced one blow after another and this was another one blooming large at her ! She did not wish to spend the rest of her life, entering a bleak house. The only way out was to concede to Krishnan's proposal of staying with him. He was feeling sick and tired quite often.

Right now, he was the only soul much concerned about her! She decided to spend the rest of her life doing service to him by cooking and cleaning up. God had been very cruel to her. He had closed one door after another! But she was determined to enter the one which was open right now! She did not wish to care about what the people would say! The past was gone and beyond redressal! She did not wish to think about the future which was unknown to her! In fact, having lost all hope that her son would take care of her, she felt very scary of the future! She wished to live for the present moment and go by the commands of her mind! Suddenly, she felt that by accepting Krishnan's proposal, he would be of great help in mitigating her fears of the future!

Lakshmi stepped into the temple, with great anxiety. Today, she was going to make Krishnan, happy and bring some joy in his life. But as she reached the spot where Krishnan would be waiting for her, after his prayers everyday, Lakshmi's heart started pounding faster. For Krishnan was not there! Frantically, she came round the temple looking for him. He was not to be seen anywhere! Then she remembered! Last evening Krishnan had complained of chest pain and he had also left early. A sudden fear gripped her mind now ! Was he alright now ? Did he go to the doctor or not ? And instantly an worst fear crossed her mind! Did he suffer an heart attack ! With her heart in her mouth, she walked hastily towards his house! On reaching his house, she pressed the calling bell and waited with abated breath ! The door opened and she saw an young girl standing there. The girl greeted her with a warm smile and asked, "are you Ms.Lakshmi ?" Lakshmi continued to stand outside with a look of apprehension on her face and finally the girl invited her in with the words, "father told me that you would be coming to see him !"

Lakshmi realized that the young girl was Krishnan's daughter.

Accompanying the girl, Lakshmi said, "your father did not come to the temple today, and I just came to find out if anything is wrong with him !"

The girl continued, "Last night, father phoned up and complained of chest pain. He feared that he was going to get an heart attack. Immediately I rushed to see him, leaving my baby with my mother-in-law!"

On hearing Lakshmi's voice, Krishnan sat up bolt upright on the bed and called out to her zealously. As Lakshmi sat on the chair close to the bed, Krishnan said, "I was really scared out of my wits last night ! The pain was unbearable and I thought I would die of an attack. That is why, I immediately rang up my daughter in Bangalore and she rushed to see me. This morning, she took me to the hospital and the doctors carried out all the tests ! According to the reports, everything is normal and the pain was due to acute Gastritis. They have just prescribed some pills and advised me to take rest ! I am feeling better now !"

Heaving a sigh of relief, Lakshmi reprimanded him, "You must start eating timely meals from now on and also follow a strict diet".

"But who is there to care for me ! My daughter is planning to leave tonight and after that I will have to do my own cooking !"

Leaving them alone, Krishnan's daughter excused herself to the kitchen to make some tea. Lakshmi decided to use this opportunity in talking about her son's letter. Shoving the letter into his hands, she said, "in fact, I had been dying since morning to meet you and show you this letter ! It is from my son !" Krishnan's face lit up with a smile as he took the letter from her. "So, at last, your son is returning to India !", he said, as he started reading the letter. But after he was finished with it, he felt sorry to have spoken like that. "I am sorry Lakshmi ! Your son has indeed been ruthless in abandoning you like that ! It is a great shock to me and I know how much this should have pained you ! And if you permit me, I shall talk to your son right away !"

But Lakshmi refused and she said, "Love should come naturally and one cannot buy it or get it under compulsion !" "If he feels happy with his wife, let him enjoy his life !"

Just then, his daughter entered with tea and handing one cup to Lakshmi, she said, "since, I have left my baby at home, I am planning to leave now ! When I requested father to accompany me to Bangalore, he says that he is feeling comfortable now !" Then hesitantly, she beseeched, "I am afraid, if I can request you to stay for a few days and cook for father ! Somehow, I don't feel like leaving him alone when he is rather sick !" But her father cut in, "Lakshmi has her own problems and I think we should not disturb her now !"

But Lakshmi stood up and walked to the young and worried girl ! Patting her on her back, she said, "you don't have to worry about your father ! Go back home peacefully and I shall take care of him !" The girl thanked her for her assurance. Lakshmi did all the chores and took great care of him. In fact, she gave her body and soul in taking care of him by fussing over him from dawn to dusk as though he were a small child. Krishnan was reminded of his own mother, who would make a great hubhub whenever he fell sick. Krishnan's health was improving by leaps and bounds and within a few days, he was back to normal.

One morning, not finding Lakshmi in his vicinity for a long time, Krishnan went around from one room to another, in search of her. Finally he saw her in the drawing room. Lakshmi was packing up her things to leave. She was not aware of the fact that Krishnan was standing at the doorway, watching silently as she was busy folding the clothes and arranging them in her bag, with her back to him. As she lifted her heavy bag and turned around, she was rather shocked to see Krishnan blocking her way, leaning on the door. With a pleading look, he asked, "should you leave this child alone and go away ?"

While Lakshmi was standing there in silence, thinking of an apt reply to give him, Krishnan grabbed the bag from her hand and walked up to his bed room. After placing it on his bed he came towards her. Holding her hands, he implored, "Lakshmi, I have been cherishing a love for you, eversince I set my eyes on you ! I admire your courage and feel strong in your presence! Both of us are sailing in the same boat and are trying our best to kill boredom and loneliness. We have just one life to live and let us not bow down to Fate, and lead a random and purposeless life !"

From the bottom of her heart, Lakshmi too, had been revering him, and also craving for his love, but at the same time, she was not dare enough to reveal it to him !

Seeing her pensive and dazed look, Krishnan continued, "don't be afraid to take a leap in the dark ! For I assure you that I shall always be present by your side and take care of you!" Lakshmi was carried away by his soothing words! She plunged into this affair not bothering about the repercussions; for she had no say in the matter!

18

The Pampered Child

Prema just turned around in her bed, when all of a sudden, she saw that the light in her daughter's bedroom was still burning. She looked at the clock and it was already past midnight. Thinking that Nithya might be preparing for her examination, she closed her eyes and tried to sleep. But sleep did not come to her. This time she was disturbed by a sniffling sound emanating from her daughter's room. She wondered if anything was wrong with her daughter! For, she had been watching her daughter's queer behaviour in the recent past and she could smell something fishy. Nithya remained despondent and was out of her element ! Her usual cheerfulness was also missing! Apart from that, she did not eat well too! More than anything else, she did not share any news about Vijay with her ! Prema got down from the bed and drowsily walked to her daughter's room to find out everything.

Numerous reference books lay scattered across the table and Nithya sat in front of them, staring at them blankly. Howmuchever she strived, she could not concentrate on her studies. She tried to fall asleep, but sleep would not come to her either and so she sat there simply sobbing - thinking of the dreadful future that was in store for her. How she had herself been the master of her own fate that was the cause of her dwindling peace of mind ! If only she had heeded to her mother's advice!

On seeing her mother enter the room, Nithya's muffled sniffles suddenly turned into loud sobs. Holding her mother's hand, she said, "mother, I am utterly confused ! I feel that God has set a trap for me and I am unable to free myself from it. I don't understand why God has punished me in this manner! Only you can help me from this mess I have got into!"

Her mother had never before seen her daughter cry like this and she became rather worried and panicky as to what was wrong. Neither was she able to understand head or tail of what Nithya was talking about and wiping her tears with her saree pallu, she consoled, "tell me what exactly is bothering you ! There is no problem in this world that has not got no solution!" Nithya then started to divulge the entire story that had been bothering her for the past six months.......

It has been rightly said that love is a very strange feeling for it happens at the odd moments and with odd people ! That turned out true in case of Nithya ! For Vijay, one of the most disgustingly attractive and handsome boy of her class was the heartthrob of every girl who set eyes on him. But it so happened that he did not pay any attention to any of them! However, for reasons unknown to himself, he was carried away by the quiet and taciturn nature of Nithya. Nithya was a bookworm and a studious girl and though she liked Vijay and also spoke to him whenever he spoke to her ; unlike other girls, she did not have any crush on him. As and when an opportunity arised, Vijay tried to strike a conversation with Nithya. Slowly, Nithya too found him irresistible and was drawn to him. She fell into the trap of love too! During the final year, Vijay proposed to her and she only accepted his proposal at once, without any second thoughts.

However, Nithya decided to tell her parents about it and not keep it a secret. Vijay had no problem in convincing his parents for they gave their consent immediately when their only son expressed his willingness to marry Nithya. But when Nithya conveyed her love affair to her parents, they made a great hue and cry over this. They told her that it was all infatuation and advised her not to get carried away by this. They further advised her to concentrate on her studies and finish her examinations first.

But Nithya was upset over this. The fact that her parents did not view her love seriously hurt her very much. She stopped talking to them. When this did not have any effect, she refused to eat at home. Depressed by the fact that their only daughter was morose and starving, finally, they relented. They spoke to Vijay's parents in this regard, and they readily agreed to wed their son to Nithya. However, they warned their children that, right now, they were to concentrate on their final year examination and once it was over, they could fix up a marriage date.

Very soon, the news of Nithya and Vijay's love affair and the fact that they were going to get married, spread across the college campus. Her friends congratulated her and told her that she was one of the luckiest girl on earth for she was going to be married to a very attractive man. They also teased her that they were really jealous of her !

Now that their parents had assented for their marriage, Vijay started taking liberties with her ! Every evening, after college was over, he would insist that she accompany him to the nearby park or the beach and both would spend an hour together, before reaching home. At first, Nithya protested and refused under the pretext that it was not proper to meet like this before wedding ; but Vijay convinced her that since they were going to be married afterall, there was nothing wrong in it !

Slowly, Nithya looked forward to these outings with him with great enthusiasm; when they could chat to their heart's content! Vijay would treat her with a pizza or a cool drink every evening, after which, he would drop her at the busstand. On reaching home, Nithya would share the news of the fun and frolic she had with Vijay and her mother would be all ears to her!

But very soon, Nithya found out the true colours of Vijay ! He was a bellicose and an irascible person. He sulked at each and everything she did and Nithya found his character so unpredictable and perplexing! Vijay nagged her whenever she committed a fault, be it anything. She was bewildered by his strange behaviour and could not believe if it was the same old Vijay who was behaving like this.

Of late, Nithya dreaded going to college ; for she hated seeing Vijay, who was nitpicking every action of hers. In fact, Vijay was becoming too much possessive of her and was always keeping watch on her like a hawk. He did not like it, if Nithya ever spoke to the opposite sex. He would yell at her, if he ever saw her speaking to any of the boys in the class room. Even if Nithya tried to clear her doubts from the male lecturers, Vijay's face would flush red with anger and in the evening, when they were alone, he would accuse and slander her, as though she had committed a great blunder !

Being the only child, Nithya was so much pampered by her parents. She detested if anyone ever tried to control her. The fact that Vijay was sceptical of her and watching all her moves and commenting about everything she did or spoke, was getting on her nerves. On her birthday, she wore a very grand churidhar and all her friends gave her presents and appreciated her dress in particular!

Vijay's behaviour on that day was really shocking to Nithya ! For not only did he not wish her on her birthday, but he also hurt her by telling, "You have come so glamorously dressed to the college today! Whom are you trying to attract now ?" Actually, it was for Vijay that she had dressed like that! She expected that Vijay would be full of praise for her and also anticipated a wonderful gift. But her expectations only ended in smoke ! And Vijay's sharp and nasty words only brought tears to her eyes. Without as much as exchanging a word with him, she silently left the place. Realizing that Vijay was always angry with her whenever she wore attractive clothes, bangles or bindis, Nithya slowly gave up wearing all these to the college, and tried to come as simply dressed as possible !

One day, during the lunch hour, Nithya was chatting with her friends inside the class room. A few boys were also sitting close by. Shortly, Vijay returned from the canteen after having his lunch and he also joined them. All of sudden, Nithya's dupata dropped off from her shoulders and immediately she bent down and picked it up, feeling very embarrassed. From his wild gaze, she knew that Vijay was going to give her a good dressing down in the evening, when they chanced to be alone. So, she skipped the rest of the classes and went home with the pretext of severe headache !

However, she was not spared from his rough behaviour! For the next day, the first thing in the morning, Vijay met her and asked her to follow him to the ground. And then he began his tirade, "have you forgotten your manners ? Yesterday, why did you run away without even informing me?" Nithya fearfully, revealed the truth that she had been scared of him. And with a wicked smile on his face, he said sarcastically, "I just can't believe what I am hearing ! If that was so, you would have pinned up your dupattas neatly, as I have been often advising you to do so! You enjoy doing things against my wishes and try to provoke me all the time! Who knows; you might have in fact intentionally let your duppatta fall off, in order to give a free show to every body present there!"

Nithya stood there gaping at him in shock ; for she was affronted by his rudeness ! Hot tears welled up in her eyes and wiping it off with her handkerchief, she cursed him, "I have never seen a sadist person like you in my life! You always enjoy inflicting pain on others! I really hate you for this! You will surely be punished by God for hurting my feelings in this manner!"

Her sharp words infuriated him further and immediately he jerked her hand severely and Nithya squirmed in pain ! "Very soon, you are going to marry me and I don't like any of the boys in the class lingering around you ! And in case if you do so, you had it !" He threatened her. Just then, one of her friends was coming towards her and quickly Nithya wrenched herself from his hold and walked away briskly from there. That day, she could not concentrate in the lectures and she remained glum for the rest of the day.

Vijay was becoming a hard nut to crack! His harsh behavior was getting on her nerves! His rudeness was eating her heart and she was not interested in the day to day affairs. She sat brooding all the time wondering about her future. However she kept her sufferings to herself and did not wish to get anyone entangled in this. She never discussed about this even with her parents nor with her close friends. Slowly, she got into a state of melancholy which reflected badly on her health too. She did not eat well and grew thin and haggard. She was always filled with a fear and completely stopped talking to the opposite sex, except her father. She stopped accompanying him in the evenings and left early with the pretext that her mother was bed ridden and she had to tend her.

But one fine day, things got rather too far. It was during the first day of the final year examination, that Nithya got to know the worst side of him. He behaved so brutally with her and Nithya knew for sure that their relationship would never be the same again! She even planned to end her relationship with him !

After writing her exam, Nithya was discussing the answers with her friends. Two of the boys of her class also joined them and were standing close to Nithya verifying with her, if their answers were right. Since Vijay had still not come out of the hall, Nithya took the liberty of talking to them at free will. She was so much engrossed in her explanation that she did not notice Vijay, who was coming towards her. And when he approached them, Nithya was still busy with clearing their doubts and only when she was done with it did she see that Vijay was standing right in front of her, searing with anger. He acted on impulse without for a moment considering as to what he was upto. He slapped her and started berating her in front of everyone. "I told you not to talk to any of the boys around, but you seem to be bent upon disobeying me! You don't have time for me in the evenings and remain gloomy all the time ! But you enjoy yourself with the rest of the boys ! Have I become so cheap to you now ?" Not wishing to start a scene, Nithya collected her books and walked away slowly towards the bus stand.............

After divulging the story to her mother, Nithya pleaded, "mother, tomorrow, I am going to pay him back in the same coin ! I am going to tell him that I no longer love him and he can go and marry someone else! He may be a very attractive person ! But what is the use of external beauty, when one's mind and heart are not pure ! I am going to severe my relations with him!"

Her mother was flabbergasted on hearing the whole story ! She knew that Nithya was so much disturbed and any word she uttered or any advice she gave, would only fall on deaf ears! For Nithya was now overwhelmed with feelings of anger and revenge. Placing her hand on her shoulders, she comforted her, "don't come to drastic conclusions, when you are angry with someone !

Let your mind cool first! Now go and sleep and you can decide about what to do, early in morning !"

But Nithya shoved her hand off and stood up. "No mother !" She said rather firmly. "I am not going to change my mind in any way ! Tomorrow, you must go and meet his parents and convey the news to them that I have ended my relationship with their son !"

Once again, her mother suggested to her, "Nithya, please don't jump to any conclusion right now ; which is your usual habit ! Just relax and go to bed! I wish to remind you once again, not to take any hasty decisions when you are angry and repent for it later on ! Don't let this incident hamper your studies! You have your exams now and you must pay attention to that! After that, you can slowly chalk out your future plan !" And she escorted her upto her bed.

But Nithya was furious and in no mood to listen to her ! She continued her grumbling, "tomorrow in the college, I am going to tell Vijay, point blank, no matter what, that I am no more interested in him! I need my freedom back ! To everyone, college life is the most enjoyable and memorable period in one's life! But to me, it is the most awful one ! After college, I wish to go for a job and enjoy life for some more time and not get tied down to marriage and family life and that too with a mad guy like Vijay ! He has insulted me in front of my friends and I am going give him tit for tat!"

While Prema returned to her bed, she mused to herself that it was all her fault ! She had pampered her daughter so much and let her have her way in all matters! She felt bad that her upbringing was basically wrong ; for they had all the while been giving in to all her whims and fancies, without raising a finger. She had always been trying to be in her daughter's good books and behaved with her more like a friend rather than a commanding and strict parent by respecting her decisions! And now she realised that she had in fact over done it! Probabaly, she thought that this was due to her selfishness ! For she feared that if she ever tried to be strict with her and have constant tiffs with her in correcting her behaviour, her daughter might try to avoid her ! She could afford to give up anything but not her daughter's love !

The next day, Nithya went to college dressed in a grand manner! She had nothing to fear anymore ! In fact, she wished that Vijay must see her and comment on her dress and she would then give him the shattering news! But many a times, things don't turn out as per our wish! For man proposes and God disposes! At times, it may be even for our own good! Nithya was in for a great shock. She had been eagerly looking around for Vijay but there was no trace of him! Even after the bell rang, Vijay did not enter the hall! And finally, when he never turned up to college, she felt awfully bad for not being able to carry out her plan ! The fact that she could not revenge him set her on edge and she was filled with rage !

Slowly, she walked up to the bus stand, wondering what could be the reason for his absence. And suddenly her thoughts were disrupted by an auto which blocked her way. She heard a familiar voice calling out her name in quick succession. Instantly she realized that it was Vijay and was swept by a wave of anger and hatred! But when her eyes fell on the huge bandage, wound across his leg from his knees, she started walking up to him. Vijay requested her to get inside the auto and she obliged.

On seeing the bandage and his dull face with a deep expression of anguish, her feelings of hatred and anger began to recede and she asked rather sadly, "did you meet with an accident or something ?"

"God has indeed punished me enough for my rude behaviour with you yesterday !" He said and started to tell her the whole story that was bugging him.

"Nithya, in fact, after our parents agreed for our wedding, I became very possessive of you and could not tolerate if people of the opposite sex approached you or spoke to you; be it our own class mates or the lecturer! You know, how the world is ! I had a fear that there might be quite a few among us who are jealous of our relationship and try to separate our love. That is why, I did not like anyone to poison your mind and take you away from me. You had been tolerating my rudeness all the while and that is why God had punished me enough. Yesterday, I had been very upset after hitting you like that. I decided that I must apologize to you. In fact, I wished to be in your house before you reached home and offer my apologies. Unfortunately, my speedy driving has resulted in a skid and I fell off the vehicle hurting my leg very badly. Luckily, I escaped with a minor fracture. The doctor has advised me complete rest for one whole month ! Nithya, I am actually mad of you and I just can't help being possessive! This character of mine probably emanates from my upbringing. I have never seen my mother leave the house any time, nor seen her talk to the neighbours ! It is my father or me, who would take care of all her requirements. To my mother, it was both of us who formed the entire world! Since I could not remain sitting at home, without seeing you, I came in an auto, against the protests of my mother ! The fact that the accident has taken place to me just after my rude behavior with you, has brought me back to my senses ! It had made me realize that I had been heartless and selfish with you all the while! Since my mother was uneducated, she remained shy, coy and withdrawn always and had to entirely depend on us! However, you are educated and bold enough to take care of all your needs unlike my mother! With your audacious and candid nature, I am sure that you would not like to exploit yourself by sitting at home like my mother, without going out for a job..........

Nithya was happy to hear his pacifical speech ! She felt joyful that Vijay had at last decided to change himself and his perceptions. She did not wish to be a silent listener and decided to air her opinions too ! Seeing that Vijay was in no way going to end his conversation, Nithya tried to interrupt him, "Vijay, you must really consider this accident as your luck ! If not for this, you would not have tried to change yourself and besides you could have also lost me for ever ! For I had been boiling inside ever since your brutal behavior yesterday and had been yearning to tell you about my decision of ending my relationship with you ! I have now changed my mind! Well, you must understand that by my dressing up fashionably or wearing glamorous dresses, I am not trying to attract anybody! It is you who came after me and tried to woo me in the first place and I have fallen into the trap! You had in fact succeeded in drawing me towards you ! Somehow, I dress up to feel good about my self which in turn gives me a little confidence while interacting with others! I am not a whore or something to just run away behind anybody who wishes to sweet talk with me! I am born and brought up in Chennai City in Tamil Nadu and hope you are aware of the culture here. It is one and only man, that a girl decides to spend her life with, however his character might be! It is not a foreign country, where marriage and love are not a life long committment! This being the age, when Indian women are vying with each other to travel in space, I was so perplexed at your strange behaviour of suspecting me whenever I spoke to the opposite sex! But I think it is God's wishes that we stay together; for by giving you this accident, he has helped me change my decision too! This accident must be considered a boon to you rather than a curse ; for it helped me change my views!" After dropping him in his house, she advised him to take complete rest and promised to visit him after her exams were over !

It was forenoon already and Prema was preparing soup for her daughter ; for it was time for her return from college after finishing the exams. As she stirred the soup, she was disappointed that her daughter would have had a tiff with Vijay and wondered how Vijay was going to take the whole thing when Nithya revealed about her drastic decision of severing her ties with him. Just as she removed the vessel of hot boiling soup from the stove with tongs and was carrying it to the dining table, Nithya excitedly came searching for her mother and almost bumped into her. Prema was really astonished to see the smile on her daughter's face. She noticed that Nithya's face was glowing with brightness, unlike in the morning and her curiosity got the better of her. "Did you meet Vijay and convey your decision?", she asked anxiously. Without answering to her question, Nithya dragged her mother excitedly to the hall. She asked her to sit on the sofa and sat down beside her.

Slowly, Nithya started to narrate to her about Vijay's accident and the abrupt change in his character. She was talking non stop in a breathless manner defending Vijay, whom she considered as a rival this morning, while Prema listened patiently to all her rantings. Then at last she said, "mother, Vijay has turned over a new leaf! I have hence changed my mind now! Since Vijay has realized his mistake, I have decided to forgive him. After all, to err is human and to forgive is divine !"

Prema was very happy! For, her daughter has now realized as to what reality is! Love life is not just a bed of roses and that heartbreaks are also a common occurrence and these are in fact important for growth. She returned with a small bowl of soup and handing it to Nithya, said, "God's will be done, Nithya ! You must understand that getting entangled in love and marriage is not as easy a task! It is a unique relationship, and you cannot break this bond at your own whim and fancy! It is a life long commitment and one need to compromise a lot ! It is often wise and best to just let things go, even though it may require an almost superhuman level of tolerance! You are no more a child, Nithya! Only a child discards a doll if it despises it! But Vijay is the man you wish to marry and with whom you will have to spend the rest of your life! I did have a premonition that you won't be able to sever your relationship with him that easily by conveying your opinion right across his face. In marriage, we have to give up many a times, in order to lead a successful life !"

For the first time, Nithya sat bemused, listening to her mother, without countering her ! She knew better than any one else, that her mother was right after all !

19

The Immatured Girl

Pooja was carefully threading the needle to commence her embroidery work. Once done with the job, she continued with her chain stitch. She was so eager to finish the design today and she was working rather enthusiastically. She was suddenly disturbed by the sharp shrill of the door bell. Thinking that it should be another sales representative, trying to sell his product, she got irritated. She continued with her work without making a move. Once again, the bell rang and since her mother was busy in the backyard, she stood up and with a frown on her face went to open the door! And when she saw the person who was standing at the door, she almost froze in shock. In fact, she became dumbfounded and words failed her ; for she never expected that he would come here, looking for her ! Without as much as exchanging a word with him, she ran to the backyard, to inform her mother. Her mother was wringing the clothes, when she saw Pooja running towards her with great anxiety. When Pooja told her about the visitor at the door, she almost dropped the clothes on the ground and followed her briskly, reprimanding her for not having manners, "Why did you not ask him to come in ? Afterall, he is your husband ! Should you come running like a small child, as though you have seen a ghost !"

But Pooja was not scared of ghosts ! For she did not believe in them! But she did not expect that her husband would come looking for her ! For, he should have surely been appraised of everything that had happened during his absence! The fact that he had come inspite of that was more perplexing to Pooja ! Pooja's heart began pounding faster and her mind was filled with several questions. What was he upto? Was he going to use his authority as her husband and beat her black and blue for what she had done? Or was he going to divorce her for running away from home? Or was he going to sweet-talk her into accompanying him back to that hell ? She was utterly confused! Instantly, she made up her mind! Whatever be the case, she was not going to leave her house! Filled with an acute sense of fear, she clung to her mother for protection !

Pooja had been a very happy and carefree girl just two months back. After completing her plus two exams, she was enjoying her holidays. But all her plans of joining college was shattered. For one evening, her maternal uncle dropped in to their house with a marriage proposal. Pooja's mother was tempted with the alliance, as the boy worked in Dubai and she felt that her daughter could lead a rich life. She agreed to this proposal immediately and without even consulting her daughter, expressed her willingness to go ahead with it. But when Pooja heard of it, she protested and told her mother that she wished to continue with her studies. However, her mother convinced her, "look here Pooja ! Why are girls reading in the first place ? So that they get a good job and be able to lead a comfortable life! These days, unless you have a well paid job, no man desires to marry you! But, now God is providing you with a nice opportunity! Even without having to go to college or a job, you can get married to a rich man, for he wants a simple and homely girl who could cook well and take care of the house! You can learn at any age, by enrolling yourself in a evening college and continue with your studies even after marriage, for learning is a continuous process! Hope, you don't deny the opportunity that knocks at your door!" Though Pooja knew that her mother was right, she sat there gloomily without replying to her. Her mother then continued, "if you agree to this alliance, you would be spared the burden of going out for a nine to five job and simultaneously carrying out household chores ! Moreover, I was also told that the boy is of very good character and is a teetotaler ! It is hard to find boys with good manners these days! If you agree to this alliance, you would be happy for the rest of your life !" Finally, Pooja nodded her head to this alliance!

She felt sad at the thought of leaving her mother. Pooja tearfully bid goodbye to her and went to her mother-in-law's house situated in a remote village in Tirunelveli. On reaching home, Dilip told her that after ten days, he would be flying to Dubai all alone on single status. He had applied for a quarters and once the same was sanctioned, he would come back and take her. On hearing, this, Pooja expressed her interest in staying with her own mother rather than with her in-laws. But

Dilip cajoled her, "it is only a matter of two months! After that I would be taking you along with me to Dubai ! My mother wishes that you stay with her during this short period and I have consented without enquiring you ! So, please stay here with them!" Pooja reluctantly agreed for the same.

But the moment Dilip left for Dubai, Pooja realized that everyone were behaving with her in an indifferent manner! Her mother-in-law, being a Diabetic patient was always lying in bed and depended on Pooja to carry out all the petty jobs for her. She would be calling out her name once in every five minutes asking her to carry out some errand or the other for her. Once, she would ask her to switch on the fan and after a little while, she would tell her to turn it off with the pretext that she was feeling cold.

To add to that, her widowed sister-in-law along with two of her boys were also living with them. On the very first day, after Dilip left for Dubai, she told Pooja, "you are so lucky to get a nice husband like my brother! Very soon, you would also be going to Dubai! I now request you to help us in taking care of the household chores! I am really fed up of doing all the house work from dawn to dusk. Hope you look after everything as long as you are here! By doing so, you would get used to our way of cooking!" Pooja had nodded her head, with the presumption that she would be around to help her out! But she had guessed wrong! For, as soon as Pooja prepared breakfast, with the instructions given by her mother-in-law, she would feed her two sons first! Then, after having hers, she would accompany them to school and while away her time with her friends. She would return late in the afternoon to have lunch. And after having a short siesta, she would leave again, this time to bring her kids from school! And Pooja remained all alone in the house, slogging the whole day. For when she was not in the kitchen cooking, she would be with her mother-in-law, helping her with some chores she had given. At other times, she would be at the backyard, washing the vessels or the clothes which the children had carelessly strewn around, after collecting them from each of the rooms. Pooja felt that she was treated no less than a servant maid in this house. Whenever, her spirits turned low because of this ill-treatment, she would say to herself, that it was afterall a matter of only two months and hence would put up with everything, in order to be in the good books of her in-laws.

But as days passed by, she realized that her body was not cooperating with her mind! It ached so much and in the nights she would keep writhing in pain, crying all alone, till sleep overtook her! Sometimes, she would even wish that the dawn should never come!

One day, she forgot to add salt to the dishes and this infuriated her sister-in-law so much that she started screaming at Pooja, "my brother is a gourmet and he has all the while been dreaming to get married to a girl who is a good cook! Poor fellow, with your cooking, he surely is going to be deceived!" Pooja pocketed the insult without retorting.

On one occasion, she was just trying to remove the hot water pot from the stove when all of sudden it slipped out of her hand and part of the hot water fell over her leg. She screamed in pain. Instead of coming to her aid, her sister-in-law only rebuked her, "has your mother not taught you anything ? You still seem to be behaving like a child ! My poor brother is going to have a tough time with you!" That night, when she went to bed, Pooja cried her grief away burying her head into the pillow all the while wishing that she must never wake up to see the dawn!

Though Pooja had been staying with them for just a month, it seemed ages to her! She could not tolerate the nitpicking attitude of her in-laws and wished to somehow escape to her home. For, she could in no way talk to her husband and confess her problems she was facing here, during his absence. Every Saturday night, Dilip rang up to talk to his wife. Pooja would not be able to express her mind to him and she would only keep answering him in monosyllables. And a crazy thought would pass her as she spoke to her husband ! She would wish that by some magic power, her husband must be able to decipher whatever was in her mind by just listening to her voice! Her mother-in-law and sister-in-law along with her two sons would be eagerly waiting to grab the phone from her hands, each requesting him to buy this or that during his return from Dubai. With so many people around her, Pooja never felt like talking to her husband for more than a few minutes.

The fact that Dilip never spoke to her about the allotment of quarters was a matter of concern for Pooja. She did not know if he was taking any steps in this direction or not ! The turmoil and hard work was telling upon her health ! She grew thin and pale and was completely worn out. She was not having time to go out and make friends with her neighbours and so she could not share her grief with others. However, as she washed the clothes in the backyard every afternoon, the servant maid of the opposite house would just come and chat with her for a few minutes and Pooja did not think it befitting to share her sufferings with that lady.

One fine morning she was all alone at home. Her in-laws had gone to attend a marriage function and informed her that they would return only late in the night. Pooja had refused to accompany them with the pretext that she had severe headache. After seeing them off, Pooja ran inside the house with great enthusiasm. She wished to phone up to her mother and her husband and divulge all about her sufferings and ill-treatment that she was undergoing in this house.

As she dialed the number, and waited for the response, she was almost shocked to hear the recorded voice, "this facility is not available on your telephone!" She almost pulled out the wire in anger and disabled the phone. Her cruel in-laws had cleverly locked up the phone before their departure. Suddenly, she decided to escape from here! She wanted to go back to her mother! But there was not a single pie with her and this irritated her even more!

She walked up to the backyard with tear suffused eyes, not knowing what to do! On one side was a huge quantity of utensils to be scrubbed and washed. On another side was a bucket full of dirty clothes to be washed. She had not had anything for breakfast for she did not feel like cooking for herself. She was in no mood to carry out any of the chores. However, she was answerable to her in-laws when they returned from the marriage function. She had also to explain the reasons for disconnecting the phone wire. A sharp anger combined with her utter helplessness was getting on her nerves. She wished to be away from this place, no matter what ! She was engulfed with a suicidal thought. Suddenly she decided to end her life! For that was the only way she could free herself from all the troubles!

That way, she could teach all of them a lesson! First her mother, for getting her into this predicament, by getting her married so soon in life! Second her husband, for leaving her in the midst of a group of malicious people, and finally her in-laws for the ill-treatment they meted out to her everyday. She wished to hang herself ! As if that was an easy way to end one's life ! She started to look around for a thick jute rope. Not finding one in the vicinity, she walked up to the servant lady, in the neighbouring house and requested her for a thick rope. The innocent woman was not aware of the purpose as to why she was asking her for a rope, and she started looking around for the same. She was successful in finding one in the nearby dump. Since it was covered with mud, she brought it near the well to wash it. Handing it over to her, she asked, "is this enough ?" Pooja grabbed it from her and walked back briskly to her house !

Kannan was feeling out of sorts! His mother was away to visit her relatives for a few days. He was alone at home. The meals he had in the hotel last night had got him into stomach problems. He was feeling very lonely with no one at home and he was expecting his mother to return very soon. Probably, he must heed to her advice and get married soon. Right now his stomach was so upset and he decided not to go out for work. He wanted to take a few antacid tablets and so after writing down the name in a bit of paper, he came out to call his servant maid and send her on this errand. But he retracted his steps, when he saw that she was busy near the dump prodding something. He was also surprised to see Pooja standing beside her. This morning, by coincidence, he had seen her family leave in an auto. Now on seeing Pooja, he wondered why this girl had not accompanied them. And on seeing her walk back vehemently with a thick rope, doubts began to assail his mind, for there was no well in her house!

Pooja threw the rope on to the fan and curled it into a loop. She pulled a stool and gently climbed over it. Suddenly, she felt a strong hand drag her out from there. Khannan's doubts were now confirmed! In her nervousness and anxiety to carry out her job perfectly, Pooja had forgotten to bolt the door inside. Nor was she aware of the fact that Khannan was following her meekly. On seeing Khannan standing in front of him, Pooja was dazed! Before she could speak a word, Khannan slapped her so hard that she swooned on the nearby bed, after letting out a loud wail! Taking the rope from there, he left the place silently.

After nearly, an hour, panic gripped him. Pooja had swooned on the bed, when he hit her. He wished to know what she was doing now. He re-entered the house once again and he saw Pooja sitting at the edge of the bed sobbing like a child. Handing over the towel he found on the bed, he said, first wipe your tears and stop crying like a child. Pooja did as he ordered her to do. Then he asked her, "you have such a nice man as your husband! Why did you ever think of ending your life in this manner ?" Pooja remained silent, without answering him. Once again, he coaxed her, to tell him the reasons for doing so. Pooja knew that he would not budge from there, until she revealed the truth to him. And slowly, Pooja let the cat out of the bag. She told him how her in-laws were ill-treating her day by day. On hearing her story, his heart melted. His own younger sister was living a horrible life with a nagging mother-in-law. But whenever, she came home with a sulky mood, complaining, he would give her brotherly advice and ask her to return home telling that things would turn better one day. Now on hearing Pooja's story, his heart melted. Immediately he asked her to pack up her things and get ready. Further, he gave her some money and accompanied her to the busstand and asked her to go happily to her mother's house. Pooja felt elated that she was leaving the hell and decided never to return to this place again. Before leaving, she requested him, "please don't reveal this attempt of suicide to any body" and Khannan promised to do so!

When her in-laws returned home, they were shocked to find the house locked. They looked around for Pooja but she was not there anywhere. Finally, they went to Khannan's house and asked him if they had seen Pooja anywhere! Khannan handed over the key to them and said, "she has left to her mother's place this morning. Before leaving, she handed over this key to me!" So saying, he gave the key to them. He did not say a word other than this. However, he decided not to keep his promise he had given to Pooja. He had to reveal everything tooth and nail to his friend Dilip and it would only do her more good than bad! For if he did not apprise the truth to her husband, he would be failing in his duties. When they entered the house, they found it in shambles. The vessels were all scattered around and the clothes lay unwashed. Dilip's mother was almost dumbfounded at the behaviour of her soft natured daughter-in-law. "I knew from the beginning that the girl was pampered a lot and her upbringing is not good ! She is not the right match for my son ! How dare she run away like this, without informing us in advance. Dilip is going to have a very tough time with her!"

When Pooja's mother saw the dull face of her daughter, she knew that something sinister had happened. As she entered the house, Pooja started to cry and pleaded with her mother, "please don't send me back to that house again !" In a painful voice, her mother asked, "what the hell has happened to you Pooja! I had been all the while thinking that you were enjoying your marital life for you had not even cared to phone up to me even once during this one month period. And where is your husband ?" Pooja then explained everything in detail to her mother. Her mother had no say in the matter. She told Pooja that she could stay here with her but once her husband dropped in to pick up her, she had to accompany him. And Pooja too agreed to her request. However, Pooja knew that he would not come and take her back. For her inlaws would have poisoned his mind.

And now after just a few days, when Pooja saw her husband standing at the door step, she was almost dumbfounded. She did not dare to speak to him and hence immediately ran to the backyard to inform her mother about his arrival. Pooja's mother invited her son-in-law and asked him to be seated in the sofa. Immediately she went in and started wheedling Pooja to go and talk to her husband and not evade him in this manner. It took her a few minutes in cajoling her and finally she relented reluctantly. Slowly, she ambled her way to the hall and positioned herself in front of him, with a neutral expression on her face. Pooja's mother was of the firm belief that being married was altogether a different experience and initially young couples do have problems adjusting to each other! It is upto them to tackle their differences and sort them out. However, it is these initial trifles that are the basis for a strong marital life later on. She did not wish to interfere in any manner and take sides. Moreover she felt rather embarrassed to be in their midst, while they had a lot to discuss and solve their problems. Hence she stealthily entered the kitchen, leaving them alone, with the pretext that she had to attend to the cooking !

The moment Dilip saw his mother-in-law leave, he held Pooja's hand and drew her close to him.

"Why did you run away like that after seeing me?" he scolded her.

Pooja looked askance at him for she had no guts to look him straight in the eye. He was looking very belligerent and his eyes were blazing with anger. She was afraid that any answer she gave him would only provoke him further and so she stood in silence, turning her face away to avoid his gaze.

Dilip then continued his tirade, "am I a Lion or a Tiger to pounce and devour you up ?"

Pooja realized that he was bent upon taking her to task for everything she did and was in no way going to let her go scot free. He was now examining her face and obviously waiting for some sort of a reaction. Pooja felt that it would be better to confess everything to him rather than maintaining a sullen silence, thus enhancing his speculations about her and arousing his anger.

Slowly she mumbled, "in fact, it is your family members that I am really scared of ! And on seeing you, I thought that you had come to take me back with you ! That is why I ran to the backyard to warn my mother not to send me along with you !"

Dilip just shrugged off her reply and snapped, "Pooja, please don't talk like that! I know it is my fault for leaving you alone with my people! You must not forget that girls do have their scuffles and difference of opinion, once they get married and enter a new family. It is natural that they do feel like a fish out of water! But it is only a matter of time and slowly they learn to swim against the tide in the rough waters of married life! However, nobody tries to end their life for that !"

Pooja was stumped. She could not believe her ears! She had pleaded with Khannan several times not to reveal about her suicide attempt to anyone! Khannan had also promised to keep it a secret! But now, he had betrayed her! The fact that her husband came to know of it was too much for her to bear! "Did that awful friend of yours unfold everything to you ?" She asked with eyes registering hurt. "Though he had promised me to keep this a secret, he has sneaked everything to you and has let me down !" Her eyes were welling up with hot tears and she sniffled louder than she intended to.....

Gesturing her to sit down beside him, Dilip said, "come on Pooja ! I very well know that you acted on impulse out of spitefulness of my people, without for a second bothering about the consequences! You are so immature and hence took a drastic decision! Whatever has happened is beyond repair and there is no use repenting for it now. Just forget it now! But stop being cross with my friend ! He has not only saved you from the jaws of death but has also been instrumental in my coming here to take you back to Dubai !"

Pooja was astonished. Wiping her tears with the back of her hand, she stared at him disbelievingly. Dilip then continued, "last Saturday, when I phoned up, my mother and sister were vying with each other to talk to me about you! They had too many complaints about you and their bickerings provoked me to a great extent. I sat there wondering how to tackle the problem at hand. In fact, I was thinking of phoning up your mother and railing her for her poor upbringing ! Just then, Khannan rang up and appraised me about the true version of the story. He cleared my mind of all the confusions and immediately I took a decision of coming over here and taking you back along with me! I also decided not to leave you alone with my family members hence forth !"

She realised that Khannan had indeed been right when he told her that she had got one of the best man as her husband. Though he admonished her for her dastardly act in trying to end her life, she could see that he was doing so out of much concern and love for her and not in any way to belittle her! She decided to accompany her husband and begin her life with a clean slate !

Slowly, her heart which had been thudding against her rib-cage, eversince his arrival returned gratefully to its familiar rhythm!

20

The Modern Wife

When Shobha heard the car screech to a halt, her heart began to palpitate. She had taken a bold step without even consulting her husband and resigned her classy job with a pay packet of Rs. 40,000/- p.m. Somehow, she had been able to explain everything to her mother-in-law this afternoon, who had taken the whole thing very cooly! But now, she was scared stiff and was worried as to how her husband was going to react on hearing the news! But once again she reassured herself that she had taken this decision, because of the love she cherished for this family ! And moreover, she wished to start a family of her own ! And for this, she had no other go but to take such a drastic step ! She now geared up herself to face the storm............

If today, Shobha had risen to this position, she owes it all to her husband. Three years back, she was just an ordinary Arts Graduate. After getting married to Ravi, everything changed in her life! Ravi was determined to transform her into a IT professional and a computer wizard! Ravi had always longed to marry a modern girl who was a professional! But his mother stood on the way! Ever since she had set her eyes on Shobha; about whom, she had learnt from her neighbor, she was determined to get her son married to her! Though Ravi refused in the beginning, he finally relented because of his mother's constant counseling! Everyday she would brainwash him, "modern girls are not suitable for you ! They would not respect you and hardly obey you ! Besides, they would prefer a lot of independence, and you would often get into frequent ego clashes ! Are you not aware that men who marry professional and well employed girls, divorce very easily due to incompatibility ? On the other hand, the girl I have seen for you is so innocent and I am sure that she will be obedient and take good care of you. You can any day, if you so desire, educate her and make her a professional, after marriage. She is just Twenty Three years old and has got the entire life before her!" That is how, she was able to convince Ravi and get him married to the girl of her choice !

Ravi had never done anything against his mother's wish! Without any regrets, he married Shobha with the sole aim of changing her into a modern and professional girl and also planned to send her for a job! After all, Ravi was already running a computer centre and imparting training including web designing to youngsters! Was it going to be difficult to educate his own wife? So, immediately after marriage, he told her about his intention. He informed her that he would give her all the coaching and make her a computer wizard.

But Shobha took the whole thing very lightly ! Born and brought up in a Village, her parents had believed that more than the education, it was the experience in cooking and house work that really mattered! Her mother had taught her all about cooking and housework. Hence, she had entered the house with the mission of carrying out her responsibility of a daughter-in-law without grumbling and to the satisfaction of all. On the first day itself, despite the protests from her mother-in-law, Shobha asked her to rest and commenced cooking. While having meals, Ravi appreciated her excellent cooking and said, "well, you cook as good as my mother. But there is no necessity for you to take over this job from her so early ! My mother is hale and healthy and she enjoys doing that job. Please leave it to her. Also, I do not like to see you spend the whole day toiling with housework. Nor do I want you to be lolling in front of the television watching the serials. I plan to teach you computer very shortly and so get ready for that !"

Within a fortnight, a brand new computer arrived home. And immediately after installation of the same, Ravi set about his task. He told her in a overbearing tone that every evening, she had to sit with him for the training and Shobha agreed to cooperate with him. Since, she had already passed typing, it was so easy for her to learn MS Word and she was easily able to type letters. She had been feeling proud that her computer training was over and that is the end of it ! But very soon, she learnt that it was a ocean and she knew just a drop of it! When Ravi started to teach her Excel, she started feeling bored. Rather she was not interested in it. She was also finding it confusing and difficult ; for it involved many formulas and tough calculations. And therefore, she did not pay much attention to it. But Ravi was in no way going to tolerate her lackadaisical attitude!

One day, he gave her an excel sheet and asked her to type it out after incorporating the formulas in it. He then left on some errand. After returning home, anxiously, he walked up to his room to find out how Shobha was faring! Ravi got tensed up when he saw that the PC was shut down and Shobha was not around. He went towards the kitchen, screaming for her.

Actually, Shobha had been sitting in front of the PC, breaking her head for a while. When she realized that she could not proceed further, she closed the computer and went into the kitchen. Ravi was rather provoked by her carelessness and he started yelling at her, "have you finished typing the worksheet I gave you ?"

Shoba cowered by his stern look and meekly drawled, "it is so difficult and I can't understand, head or tail of that !" "Stop everything and come here ! Tell me what is it that you can't understand ! I shall clear your doubts", he said as he ambled to his room. Shobha did not follow him, but instead continued to linger in the kitchen ! She kept toying with the vessels in the cupboard; dwelling on the apt manner in which she could come out of this learning business! Ravi switched on the PC and waited for her! There was no sign of her and he angrily got up to see what was holding her up! When he found her still standing in front of the gas stove, without caring to abide by his words, he was annoyed! Irately, he switched off the stove and dragged her out forcibly, shouting, "you really are an audacious woman !" Shoba accompanied him without protesting ! However, she decided to talk it out with him! For, she realized that it was now or never! She wished to tell him that she could not understand anything and more than that, she was disinterested. He ordered her to sit down.

"Now, tell me your problem", he commanded.

Picking up courage, she grumbled, "why don't you please leave me from this training! It is so tough and I am sure that I can never learn all this! You will unnecessarily be wasting your time!"

On hearing this, Ravi's anger soared sky-high! He struck her across her face and bawled, "don't ever utter such hopeless words again !"

Shoba recoiled immediately ! Without speaking a word, she got up swiftly and walked to her room in a huff. Ravi did not try to stop her.

He sat there mulling over the whole incident. One thing was crystal clear! Shobha was not cooperating with him and was not making any effort from her side to learn and acquire the knowledge, which he was so eager to impart to her. He had to somehow get her interested in this! At the same time, he also cursed himself for losing his temper. Suddenly, he realized that educating his wife was going to take some time and he had to be patient and kind with her ! Slowly, he walked up to her and sat down on the bed. Holding her arm, he yanked her to sitting position! Shobha immediately sat up sniffling and looking askance from him. Though there was a cold response from her, Ravi continued his chattering. He then apologized to her, "sorry to have hit you like that! In fact, it was your lack of enthusiasm that enraged me!" He spoke to her soothingly for a long time about his aims and goals and finally Shobha reassured him that she would take all out efforts to learn everything that he taught her.

That day, Shobha learnt, how serious Ravi was about his mission and she also realized that he was not going to let her off the hook so easily. From then on, she paid much attention to whatever he taught by taking down notes. She also sat down and practiced everything that he taught her. She did not wish to disappoint him in any manner and so strained herself to please him. And soon, she became a whiz kid. There was nothing she was not aware of in the field of computer.

One fine day, he informed her about an advertisement that appeared in the internet and asked her to apply for the job, as she was suitable for the same. It was a large multinational company on the look out for fresh graduates with computer knowledge. It was a proud moment for him, when Shobha was offered the job.

Shobha's knowledge of computers stood her in good stead. In an organization which appreciated talent, she proved her skill. Though she started with a salary of Rs. 5000/- per month, gradually, her salary rose to Rs. 40,000/- within a few years.

She equipped the house with new and latest models of television, sofa sets, fridge etc. She was now in the verge of buying a car for her husband. However, her job made her too tired and she was left with no energy to do housework. She did not find time to sit and talk to her husband like before, nor carry out any chores for him. On the other hand, her mother-in-law slogged the whole day. Ravi was missing her a lot. For she went away to work even on week ends when he was at home.

One morning, Ravi had already left to his office and Shobha was getting ready to leave. Just then, her Mother-in-Law complained about severe chest pain and requested her to inform her son about it. But Shobha had been smart enough and had immediately taken her to the hospital. When the doctor examined her, he appreciated Shobha for bringing her to the hospital at the right time for even a delay by a few minutes would have resulted in her death. He told her that she had had a massive heart attack and admitted her there. Her mother-in-law recovered slowly after a week's stay in the hospital. However, at the time of discharging, the doctor advised her that hence forth, she was not suppose to lift heavy things and should also not strain herself much.

Now, the burden of cooking and all the house work fell on Shobha and she was already beginning to feel the strain. In fact, her mother-in-law had shared half her burden in house work. But now she was finding it very difficult to cope up with the tension. She engaged a servant to take care of the cleaning job. She was then planning to appoint a cook and told her mother-in-law about it. Though her mother-in-law agreed for the same, she did not like the food prepared by the cook. Shobha was left with no option but to stop the cook. And she started getting up early in the morning to do the cooking all by herself. Also, when she returned home, it was already 8.00 P.M and she was feeling terribly tired. However, she could not even take a few minutes of rest and had to enter the kitchen to commence dinner!

Life became too hectic for Shobha. Without complaining, she went about slogging from dawn to dusk. But one fine day, she was forced to take a drastic decision. She was about to leave for work, when suddenly her mother-in-law expressed her desire to talk to her and Shobha obligingly sat down in the sofa in front of her. "My health is deteriorating day by day", she began. "My only desire now is to see a grandchild! I shall then die in peace. Since it is almost three years now, I think it is time that you give it some thought and see a doctor" she said. Shobha immediately allayed her fears by informing her that she was also concerned about this lately and had in fact already seen a doctor along with her husband. Further, she appraised everything that the doctor told her, that there was nothing wrong with them and it was her tension filled life that was delaying her from getting conceived. She rose from the sofa and dashed towards the door, after reassuring her mother-in-law that she would give her good news very soon.

On her way to work, she kept thinking if she could ever keep her promise and fulfill her mother-in-law's wish. That was when an idea struck her mind. Why not leave the job, she thought! It was due to her job, that she was unable to devote much time for her family. As per the advice given by her doctor, all that was now required for her to conceive was some rest and a relaxed mind, which would become possible only if she resigned her job. She was now bent upon having a child, no matter what. She wished to please her mother-in-law. After all, she had also been responsible for the hi-fi life that she was now leading. She had in fact cajoled her son into this marriage and that too without demanding any dowry. Also, after marriage, she had taken good care of her. When she was in good health, she had never let her do any work and attended to all the household chores all by herself. And whenever her son had angrily raised his voice at her, she would pop up from no where and ask him to cool down. And now it was her turn to fulfill her mother-in-law's wish!

Of late, she also noticed that her husband, was also getting irksome. As if he was not aware of her predicament, he often grumbled when food was not ready in time and many a times, left without having his breakfast. What was the use of money, if it could not bestow happiness to anyone ? The only solution to all her problems, she decided was to resign her job! Shobha was confident that finding a new job was not going to be very difficult. With all her qualifications, she could find a new job any time and any where...........

Though she had taken a bold decision and resigned her job; on reaching home, she was gripped with a sudden fear! She had no idea how her husband was going to take the whole thing. Was he going to resent her action or approve of it? After all, it was due to his efforts that she was able to climb the social ladder! When she had revealed everything to her mother-in-law, she took it rather lightly and remarked, "you have done the right thing. We are in no way short of money that you should strive so hard from dawn to dusk to eke out a living !"

Shobha had been rehearsing several times, as to how to break the news to her husband in a convincing manner. However, the moment she saw him, she became dumbfounded. Silently, she went inside the kitchen to prepare coffee for him. She saw hiın sitting and chatting with his mother, when she returned with the coffee cup. Mustering up courage and not wishing to beat about the bush, she told him pointblank, "I have resigned my job today!" On hearing this, Ravi was shocked and he demanded, "what for? Have you gone crazy all of a sudden ?" Before he could utter another word, her mother-in-law jumped to her rescue. She explained the reasons that induced Shobha to take such a drastic step. She justified her action by telling him that since Shobha's intention now was to have a child of her own, she had no other go but to leave her job. After hearing the whole story from his mother, Ravi only heaved a loud sigh.

Shobha was acutely sensitive to his every mood and she was instantly conscious of his displeasure. She now tried her best to open his eyes and justify her action. "you had in fact given me very good training and finding a job is not going to be so difficult for me ! I am now confident of getting a job very easily. But right now, I wish to take care of the family. I can't see you and your mother starving for food. Also, the other day - as you are also aware - the doctor has advised me that if we are to start a family, I need to relax and be free of any tensions. That's why I have resigned my job!"

Though Ravi had taken much pains to bring out the latent talent hidden deep inside her, he was probably content with the explanation Shobha had given to him. He remained silent without offering any comments. Shobha was much elated. She had expected a severe blasting from him. But there were no fireworks. For Ravi, satisfied with her rationalization had taken the whole issue very lightly and commented, "well, do as you please. I do not wish to force you to go for a job. In future, if you ever wish to go out for work, you can assist me in my training centre!" Shobha was doubly excited. She was now a free bird! She had all the time in the world to lead a life as she pleased !

However, despite all this, Ravi felt gratified that he had achieved his goal. He had in fact succeeded in transforming his wife into a modern lady. Who else would be so assertive and take such dauntless decisions!

21

The Proud Father

For a second, Karunakaran vacillated! Then taking a bold step and without any reservations, he pressed the door bell! He stood there in great anticipation, expecting to see the reaction of his daughter on finding him there! It was a moment of discomfort for Karunakaran! Six months back, when his daughter Jayalakshmi had visited him along with her baby son, he had vilified her ! Now, he was unsure whether his daughter would greet him in or turn her back on him! She had then left the house in a huff shouting at him that she wished to severe her relationship with her parents for being so rude and would never step into the house again ! Jaya was a strong willed girl who would not change her mind very easily ! For not even once during the past six months, did she try to contact her parents! And hence, Karunakaran had now come on his own; as an uninvited guest! Right now, he was very anxious to know if his welcome was going to be a warm one or whether he would receive a cold reception ....

Being the only daughter, Jayalakshmi enjoyed abundant love from both her parents. She had always had the last word in the family! Her parents had put up with her difficult nature and given in to her ways! Though her father was an ordinary clerk in a private company, he had educated her well and had gone all out to see to the comforts of his daughter! He never talked about his pecuniary problems in front of her! Jaya believed that her father was a rich man ; for all her needs were met immediately by him without as much as a murmur! He kept his problems to himself and never let his daughter know of it! He had also saved enough money for her marriage and got her married into an affluent family!

Jaya was overwhelmed with arrogance, associated with people born with a silver spoon in their mouths! After marriage, for the first time in her life, her ideas and views were being repulsed and she found it very difficult to adjust to this change! However, she never made any attempts to change her attitude ! On the other hand, her husband Ramkumar was in no way prepared to let her have the last word! He wished that his wife must be a perfect homemaker! Jaya was at variance with all that her husband expected her to do and this resulted in their frequent quarrels ! Very often, she would become sulky with a gloomy face and Ramkumar quietly avoided her at such times! Also, he never took the first step towards reconciliation and it was Jaya who after a few days of sullen silence, would go to him seeking forgiveness!

Very soon, her husband's obstinate behavior got on her nerves! Both were headstrong and this nature set them poles apart in their marital life! They constantly kept vying with each other like cats and dogs! But one fine day, when Jaya told her husband that she was pregnant, he tried to be less demanding and softened a little towards her. He never screamed if the rooms were un swept or if she failed to give him his breakfast in time! Jaya fussed a lot over her pregnancy and used this as a pretext to avoid household chores which she detested the most! When Ramkumar advised her that this was the time that she had to physically strain so as to deliver the child normally and derided her for her sluggishness, she just brushed aside his snide remarks and continued to avoid house work by engaging servant maids. And finally, when her son was born, she continued with her lackadaisical attitude without much care either for her husband or her child.

One fine day, Jaya was breast-feeding her baby, when she saw her husband enter the kitchen. When he found that Jaya had not yet commenced cooking, he was infuriated and yelled at her! "Are you going to send me to the office without giving me any breakfast?" Jaya got quickly offended by his raised voice and shot back, "can't you see that it is your son that I am attending to ? How could you be so mean ?"

"Well, take your own time, My Dear! I shall have my breakfast and lunch in the office canteen today!" He said, and started to wear his pants so as to leave early.

Jaya knew at once that he was being sarcastic and unable to bear his derisive words, she put down the baby on the bed and went into the kitchen fuming. Immediately, her son started wailing at the top of his voice. But Jaya did not care for him. She noisily cluttered the vessels in the cupboards and continued with her cooking ! Ramkumar then started to blast at her, "can't you hear the baby crying? Go and lift him up first! You can then come and cook for me!" Unmindful of his flare up, she lingered in the kitchen attending to her work. Unable to bear the screams of his son, Ramkumar forcibly drew her out of the kitchen after turning off the gas stove. And it was now Jaya's turn to bluster! "I have just got two hands and I cannot dance to your tunes! Let him cry for a while; nothing would happen to your son! And if you care so much for him, why don't you try to stop his crying by lifting him up? After all, he is your son too!" With these harsh words, she once again attempted to enter the kitchen. Provoked by her adamant behavior, he flung the powder tin across her and had not Jaya ducked at the right time, it could have hurt her badly! Getting closer to her, he commanded her to pacify the baby immediately! Scared to retort back, Jaya silently obliged !

However, Jaya could not pocket the insult ! She decided that, this time, she was not going to make any effort towards appeasing him. Later, during the day, she phoned up to her husband and informed him that she was going to her parents house with the baby ! Ramkumar knew that she was upset with him and hence was taking a drastic decision. Repentantly, he asked her when she would be returning and Jaya angrily placed the receiver on the cradle with a loud thud after replying, "only God knows that!"

When her mother saw Jaya alight from the auto struggling with the baby all alone, she ran out to receive her! Taking the baby into her arms, she came in along with her, cooing soft words to her grandson. It was after an hour that her father enquired her as to why her husband did not accompany them. Immediately, Jaya came out with her story. Karunakaran was disappointed to learn that his daughter had come off after a fight with her husband. He became restless and tried to convince her that she was in the wrong! He advised her that since she was now a mother of a child, she had to change her attitude! She had to become tolerant and patient towards everything in life! Further, he told her that it was not appropriate on her part to take offence at the slightest thing that her husband said or did and had to be broadminded and forebearing! He disapproved of her coming home after having a clash with her husband! But Jaya cared less for his ranting and decided not to return home until her son grew up a little!

While her father condemned her action, she enjoyed her mother's loving support! After three days, Ramkumar phoned up to her! When she heard his voice, Jaya cut the line as she was not interested to speak to him. In fact, she was leading a carefree life here as her mother was looking after all her needs and she did not wish to go back and slog from dawn to dusk doing the household chores, which in her opinion was a thankless job! Now that she had a baby to look after, she was finding it difficult to live up to her husband's expectations and this resulted in frequent wrangles between them !

A week had passed by and once again Ramkumar called her! But Jaya told him point blank that she would return only after six months as the baby would have grown up by then ! And this time, Ramkumar placed the phone with a thud after shouting at her that if this was the case, there was no need for her to return and she could enjoy living with her parents for ever!

However, Jaya never revealed about this conversation to her parents!

Karunakaran was leading a peaceful retired life! Although he received no pension from his company, he had wisely saved his money in fixed deposits and enjoyed the interests every month. This meager amount was sufficient to take care of the needs of him and his wife! Now with the presence of two extra hands in the family, Karunakaran was feeling the pinch! More than the day to day expenses involved, he was rather concerned about his daughter's continued stay without any talk of returning to her husband! He also worried as to why his son-in-law never came to take his daughter back.

Whenever his wife kept pestering him for money to buy this or that, either for her grandson or her daughter, he got irked and frowned at her! Though Jaya actually knew her father's predicament, she pretended not to be aware of it! But one fine day, things had gone too far!

Jaya had stopped breast-feeding when her son turned Seven months old! She started feeding him with baby foods readily available in the market. One fine day, her son was crying like hell and Jaya went to the kitchen to mix some cerelac ! She found that it was almost empty and ran and informed her mother about it. In turn, her mother went to request her father to buy cerelac! It was only then that Karunakaran had returned from the market, after purchasing vegetables. Since it was so hot outside, he was sweating a lot and so after washing up, he went and lay down in the bed for a short siesta. Just then, Jaya's mother complained to him that the cerelac was over and asked him to buy another packet immediately as the baby was famished and screaming at the top of his voice! With a frowning face, he abruptly got up from the bed and yelled at her, "look at my luck ! Even after getting your daughter married, I have to still keep spending money not only for her, but her son too! While I was rejoicing in the thought that all my financial burdens have come to an end, another one as freshly crept in from which, I believe, there is no escape for me! God has decided not to spare me till the last moment of my life !"

Jaya stood near the door fazed ; eavesdropping everything! Her father's grumbling hurt her to a great extent ! Tears welling up, she brusquely walked into her room and cried so hard! It was not right on her father to humiliate her like this ! She decided to do something about this! When her father returned in a few minutes and gave her the carry bag containing the items she required, she pulled up a long face and walked away in a huff! While her father pocketed the insult and stood there confused, Jaya returned immediately and started screaming at him, "you don't have to buy anything for my son! My son is not an orphan and he has a loving father to take care of him and he is not at your mercy! I am returning home this evening! Also, please remember ! I shall never step in to this house again and this very moment I wish to severe my ties with you !"

On hearing these sharp words, her father was dumbfounded! Only then did he realize that his daughter had in fact overhead his outburst to his wife, before leaving the house on this errand! He explained to her that it was due to fatigue that he spoke so harshly and that he had no any bitter feelings towards her ! Her mother too intervened and told her that, of late, her father was getting irksome ; probably due to age and exhaustion and requested her not to take her father's reproaches to heart ! However, their soothing words only fell on deaf ears and that evening, Jaya packed up her things and left the house along with her son !

Ramkumar was getting ready to go out to have dinner! Ever since Jaya left him, he was having his food in a nearby restuarant! When he saw Jaya and his son, he was ecstatic and welcomed them with open arms! He grabbed his son from her enthusiastically and spent the rest of the evening with him! Jaya sought forgiveness for leaving him like that! By giving up her haughtiness and through love and affection, Jaya was able to change her husband ! He softened a little and easily gave in to her wishes without being very authoritative ! Very soon, Jaya started enjoying her marital life ....

Jayalakshmi was having her bath, when she heard the door bell ! Her little son, who was sitting on the floor playing with his toys, abandoned them and trotted towards the door ; for he knew that whenever the door bell rang, there would be a visitor at the door ! Though Karunakaran had been standing outside for just a few minutes, it seemed like eternity to him! And it was only after seeing his grandson, that he realized that the door was in fact not bolted ! Immediately, he scooped up his grandson into his arms and walked in !

On hearing the muttering sound, Ramkumar came into the hall ! He invited his father-in-law with a smile! He could not thank him enough ; for it was because of his rudeness that Jaya had returned to him and not only that, but also gave up her arrogance and puffed-up behavior! While asking him to take his seat, he went in to inform his wife about his arrival ! Within a few minutes, Jaya entered the hall! Time assuages everything and so was Jaya's feelings of anger and hatred against her father! She greeted him with a warm smile and then enquired about her mother ! Immediately she excused herself and went into the kitchen to prepare coffee for her father !

While Ramkumar was giving company to his father-in-law, he openly expressed his gratitude to him ! "But for you, I would still be leading a bachelor's life !" He said. Further, Ramkumar continued, "if only all fathers are like you and behave harshly with their daughters when they go home after argument with their husbands, will there be less talk of divorce ! But hardly do parents turn down their daughters and instead encourage them, by instigating them further against their spouse, resulting in separation !"

Karunakaran only chuckled on hearing his son-in-law brag about him! For he alone knew the truth! He had in fact spoiled his daughter and pampered her a lot! Even on the day, he spoke offensively of her, it had come out of his mouth spontaneously due to exhaustion of excessive shopping he was engaged with since morning! And that too, he had expressed his frustration only to his wife and not to his daughter! Had he known that his daughter was standing nearby, he would have hardly uttered any impolite words ; for he loved his daughter more than anything else!

The whole thing, as it turned out, was a mere coincidence! He had no intention of hurting his daughter, for he loved her a lot! But then, this is what is called Fate! It is a potent force and it rules our lives! For its ways are so strange and unpredictable! However, the fact that he had been instrumental in his daughter leading a happy marital life made him elated! Further, his son-in-law's appreciation made him feel proud!

Index